Reality TV Producer

Creating a Modern Reality TV Show

Andrew Parry ©2024

This book is a must-read for aspiring reality TV producers, industry enthusiasts, and anyone curious about the fascinating world of reality television. With its comprehensive insights and insider knowledge, it offers a captivating look into the creation of this dynamic and ever-evolving genre. This book includes an analysis of 10 successful reality shows and also includes 40 ideas for new Reality TV Shows.

Introduction: The Genesis of a Modern Reality TV Show

The creation of a modern reality TV show, especially one in the realm of popular series like 'Survivor' or 'Big Brother', is an intricate process, blending real-life spontaneity with carefully orchestrated drama. These shows, while rooted in the concept of reality, are often largely scripted to heighten dramatic effect. Each episode typically revolves around a specific situation or competition, designed to engage viewers both emotionally and intellectually.

The first step in creating such a show is concept development. This phase is crucial as it sets the tone for everything that follows. The concept should be unique yet relatable, allowing viewers to see themselves in the contestants' shoes. For instance, 'Survivor' capitalizes on the human instinct for survival in extreme conditions, whereas 'Big Brother' explores interpersonal dynamics in a closed environment. The key is to find a fresh angle or a twist on existing formats that can captivate an audience.

Once the concept is solidified, the next step is casting. Casting is more than just selecting participants; it's about creating a dynamic cast that ensures a mix of personalities and backgrounds, leading to natural yet compelling conflicts and alliances. The casting process often involves extensive interviews and psychological evaluations to ensure that participants are suitable for the show's potentially stressful environment. This diversity in casting not only makes the show more interesting but also broadens its appeal to a wider audience.

Following casting, the production team focuses on scripting. While reality TV suggests unscripted content, the truth is more nuanced. Scripting in reality TV doesn't mean dictating every word and action; rather, it's about setting up scenarios and challenges that elicit certain behaviors or reactions from the cast. This scripting is subtle, often involving the layout of the environment, the type of challenges contestants face, and the timing of these events. The aim is to create situations that feel organic yet are designed to maximize drama and entertainment value.

The show's environment and set design are also critical elements. For shows like 'Survivor', this involves selecting remote, exotic locations that challenge contestants and provide visually stunning backdrops. In contrast, a show like 'Big Brother' requires a meticulously designed house equipped with cameras and microphones to capture every moment. The set is not just a physical space but a tool to influence participant behavior and, by extension, the show's narrative.

Another key aspect is the role of the host. A good host acts as a bridge between the contestants and the audience, guiding the narrative and providing context. They need to be charismatic and empathetic, capable of drawing viewers into the story. The host's interaction with contestants can also be a source of drama and entertainment, adding another layer to the show.

Once filming begins, the role of editing becomes paramount. Reality TV is made in the editing room. Hours of footage are condensed into cohesive, engaging episodes. The editing process not only involves cutting down footage but also shaping the narrative. This is where characters are built, heroes and villains are made, and stories are told. The editors play a crucial role in determining what the audience sees and how they perceive the events and participants.

Music and sound design are also vital in crafting the show's atmosphere. The right music can heighten tension, signal a mood change, or cue emotional responses from the audience. Sound effects and background scores are carefully selected to complement the visual narrative and enhance the overall viewing experience.

Marketing and viewer engagement strategies form the final piece of the puzzle. In today's digital age, this often involves a multi-platform approach, including traditional advertising, social media campaigns, and interactive online content. Engaging viewers beyond the weekly episodes through social media polls, behind-the-scenes footage, and online discussions helps in building a loyal fanbase and keeping the audience invested in the show.

In conclusion, creating a modern reality TV show is a complex, multifaceted process that requires careful planning and execution at every stage. From concept development to casting, scripting, set design, hosting, editing, sound design, and marketing, each element plays a crucial role in shaping the show's success. The end product, while presented as reality, is a carefully crafted narrative designed to entertain, engage, and sometimes even educate the audience.

Chapter 1: The Art of Reality: Conceptualizing the Show

The journey of creating a compelling reality TV show begins with a seed of an idea, a concept that can capture the imagination of millions. This initial stage, the conceptualization of the show, is both an art and a science. It requires a deep understanding of what captivates audiences, blended with creative flair. At this embryonic stage, producers and creators brainstorm ideas, often drawing inspiration from societal trends, human psychology, and existing successful formats. The goal is to create a concept that is original yet familiar, exciting yet relatable.

The art of conceptualizing a reality show involves identifying a core theme or premise that is both intriguing and sustainable over multiple episodes or seasons. This could be a survival challenge, a social experiment, or a talent contest. The key is to find a unique angle that sets the show apart. For example, 'Survivor' capitalized on the human spirit of endurance and strategy in extreme conditions, while 'Big Brother' explored the intricacies of social interactions in a controlled environment. These concepts resonated with viewers because they offered a unique lens through which familiar human experiences were magnified and dramatized.

Once the broad concept is defined, the next step is to flesh out the specifics. This includes determining the format of the show – will it be elimination-based, point-based, or will it follow another structure? The format must complement the central concept, enhancing the drama and excitement. For instance, an elimination-based format adds suspense and a competitive edge, essential for shows where endurance or talent is tested.

Another critical aspect of conceptualization is defining the target audience. Who are the viewers this show aims to captivate? Understanding the audience is crucial for tailoring the show's content, style, and marketing. It influences everything from the casting choices to the challenges designed. A show targeting young adults might focus more on social dynamics and alliances, while one aimed at a broader family audience might prioritize diverse challenges and a more inclusive cast.

Creating the rules and structure of the show is also an essential part of the conceptualization process. This involves detailed planning of how the show will operate - how will participants be eliminated? What are the rewards and penalties? How will the winner be decided? The rules must be clear, fair, and, above all, engaging. They form the backbone of the show, providing a framework within which drama can unfold.

Equally important is considering the ethical implications of the concept. Reality TV operates in a delicate balance between entertainment and exploitation. The concept must be ethically sound, ensuring that while participants may face challenges and conflicts, their well-being is always a priority. This ethical consideration extends to the portrayal of participants and the impact of the show on their lives post-broadcast.

The conceptualization phase also includes preliminary budgeting and funding considerations. Reality TV can range from low-budget, simple setups to elaborate, high-cost productions. The concept needs to be feasible within the budgetary constraints and potential revenue streams. This financial planning is crucial to ensure that the concept can be translated into reality without compromising its core elements.

Once the concept is thoroughly developed, the next step is to create a pitch. This pitch is crucial for securing funding, network approval, or partnerships. It needs to succinctly yet passionately convey the essence of the show, its appeal, and its potential for success. A good pitch not only outlines what the show is about but also why it is relevant and how it stands out in the competitive landscape of reality TV.

In conclusion, conceptualizing a reality TV show is a multifaceted process that lays the foundation for everything that follows. It requires creativity, strategic planning, and a keen understanding of the audience. The concept is the heartbeat of the show, driving its format, content, and appeal. It is the first crucial step in a journey that transforms a simple idea into a captivating reality TV phenomenon that can enthral audiences worldwide.

Chapter 2: Casting the Characters: A Diverse Ensemble

Casting for a reality TV show is a meticulous process that goes beyond simply selecting individuals; it involves curating a diverse ensemble that can bring the show's concept to life. This chapter delves into the intricate process of casting, highlighting the strategies employed to assemble a cast that not only reflects a wide range of personalities and backgrounds but also possesses the potential to create engaging and dynamic television.

The primary objective in casting for reality TV is to find individuals who are authentic, compelling, and capable of handling the pressures of the show. Unlike actors in scripted television, reality TV participants are expected to be themselves, albeit often in heightened circumstances. This authenticity is key to the audience's engagement; viewers need to believe in the characters and invest in their journeys. Therefore, casting directors look for people who are not only interesting in their own right but also able to be genuine in front of the camera.

Diversity in casting is crucial. This means a mix not just in terms of ethnicity and gender, but also in personalities, backgrounds, and life experiences. A diverse cast ensures a range of perspectives and reactions, essential for creating the kind of unpredictable and varied content that keeps viewers engaged. For instance, in a show like 'Big Brother', where social dynamics play a significant role, having participants with different viewpoints and strategies can lead to compelling alliances and conflicts.

The casting process often starts with a wide net, including open calls, online applications, and scouting. This initial phase is about gathering a large pool of potential participants from which to choose. Casting teams look through thousands of applications, searching for those individuals who stand out. Key traits include a strong presence, a compelling story, and a personality that will shine on screen.

Once potential candidates are identified, the next step is the interview process. This is where casting directors get to know the applicants, assessing not only their suitability for the show but also how they might interact with others. Interviews can range from informal chats to in-depth psychological evaluations. This helps in understanding the contestants' motivations, resilience, and how they might cope with the stress and publicity that come with being on the show.

Ethical considerations are paramount during casting. It is essential to ensure that participants are entering the show with full knowledge of what it entails and are mentally and emotionally prepared for the experience. The well-being of the cast is paramount, and responsible casting involves making sure that participants are not exposed to situations that could cause them undue distress.

Once the interviews are complete, the final selection process begins. This involves balancing personalities and demographics to create a dynamic and interesting group. The final cast is usually a mix of contrasting characters – some who are likely to form alliances, and others who might naturally clash. The aim is to create a microcosm of society, where different viewpoints and approaches to the game can come into play.

After the cast is selected, the next step is preparing them for the show. This might involve briefings on the rules and expectations, media training, and sometimes even physical or skill-based training, depending on the nature of the show. This preparation is crucial in ensuring that the participants are ready for the challenges ahead, both during and after the show.

In conclusion, casting for a reality TV show is a complex and nuanced process. It requires a keen eye for personality, a deep understanding of the show's dynamics, and a commitment to ethical and responsible selection. The cast is the heart of any reality show, and their selection sets the stage for the drama, entertainment, and emotional engagement that define the success of the series. A well-cast show can become a cultural phenomenon, with its participants leaving a lasting impression on the audience's minds.

Chapter 3: Scripting Reality: Blurring the Lines

The concept of scripting in reality TV is a nuanced and often misunderstood aspect of the genre. Unlike traditional scripted television, where actors follow a written script, reality TV involves a different kind of scripting – one that orchestrates scenarios and environments to elicit natural responses from the cast. This chapter explores how reality TV blurs the lines between reality and script, creating a unique narrative form that captivates audiences worldwide.

The core of scripting in reality TV lies in setting up situations that lead to genuine reactions. Producers and writers craft challenges, tasks, and environments that are conducive to drama, conflict, and, ultimately, entertainment. For instance, in a show like 'Survivor', contestants might be given a physically demanding task that tests their endurance and teamwork. The task itself is scripted, but the participants' reactions, interactions, and strategies are their own. This creates a dynamic where the scripted setup leads to unscripted, authentic responses.

Another aspect of scripting in reality TV is the strategic manipulation of the environment. Producers design sets and living conditions to foster certain behaviors. For example, in 'Big Brother', the house is designed to encourage interaction and confrontation. The close quarters, shared living spaces, and even the arrangement of furniture are all carefully considered to create an environment that heightens emotions and drama.

The confessionals or diary rooms in many reality shows are a prime example of semi-scripted content. While participants speak freely, they are often prompted by off-camera questions or asked to discuss specific events or feelings. These sessions provide insight into the participants' thoughts and strategies, offering viewers a deeper understanding of the dynamics within the show. They are a blend of scripted prompts and unscripted responses, adding layers to the narrative.

Editing plays a significant role in the scripting of reality TV. Editors have the daunting task of sifting through countless hours of footage to create a cohesive and engaging storyline. They decide which conversations, conflicts, and moments make it to the final cut, effectively shaping the narrative and the characters' portrayal. This post-production scripting can significantly alter the context and meaning of events, constructing a narrative that may differ from the raw reality of the recorded footage.

The use of narration or voice-over is another tool in scripting reality TV. A narrator can guide the audience's perceptions, highlight certain aspects of the story, and fill in gaps in the narrative. The tone and content of the narration can significantly influence how viewers perceive the events and characters on the show.

Producers also script interactions by casting specific types of personalities that are likely to clash or bond. This calculated mix of characters is designed to create natural tension and alliances, driving the narrative forward. The casting choices are, in a sense, a form of pre-production scripting, setting the stage for the drama that unfolds.

It's important to note that while reality TV employs these scripting techniques, the emotions and reactions of the participants are real. This authenticity is what draws viewers to the genre. People enjoy seeing real human experiences, even in a controlled and somewhat scripted environment. It offers a glimpse into the complexities of human behavior and social interaction.

In conclusion, scripting in reality TV is an art form that balances control with spontaneity. It involves creating scenarios and environments that elicit genuine reactions, shaping these reactions through editing and narration, and casting a mix of personalities to ensure dynamic interactions. This blurring of the lines between reality and script is what makes reality TV a unique and enduringly popular genre. It reflects a controlled chaos – a carefully orchestrated dance between the real and the constructed, providing entertainment that resonates with the unpredictability of real life.

Chapter 4: Setting the Stage: Designing the Show's World

In reality TV, the physical environment plays a crucial role in shaping the narrative and the experience of both the participants and the viewers. This chapter explores how the setting of a reality TV show is meticulously designed to enhance the storytelling, provoke interactions among the cast, and create a visually appealing experience for the audience.

The design process begins with a clear understanding of the show's concept and objectives. For instance, a show like 'Survivor' requires a rugged, outdoor setting that challenges the contestants and emphasizes the survival aspect. In contrast, a show like 'Big Brother' demands an intimate, closed environment where social dynamics can unfold under constant scrutiny. The setting is not just a backdrop; it's an active participant in the narrative, influencing the behavior and decisions of the cast.

In designing the set, every element is carefully considered to contribute to the show's atmosphere and objectives. In outdoor reality shows, locations are chosen for their dramatic landscapes, potential for challenges, and, importantly, their ability to be controlled and monitored for safety.

The isolation of these locations also plays a psychological role, stripping contestants of their comfort zones and placing them in an unfamiliar environment where their true personalities can emerge.

For shows set in a constructed environment, like the 'Big Brother' house, the design is even more deliberate. Spaces are designed to encourage interaction – communal areas where contestants must coexist, juxtaposed with private spaces like confessionals where they can express individual thoughts. The layout may include strategic elements like one-way mirrors or hidden rooms, adding an element of surprise and intrigue.

Technology is a significant component of the set design. Cameras and microphones are integrated into the environment, capturing the action from multiple angles without being obtrusive. The aim is to record the most authentic interactions possible. In some shows, technology is also a part of the narrative, with contestants interacting with digital interfaces or participating in tech-driven challenges.

Lighting and color schemes are other critical elements. They are used not just for aesthetic appeal but also to set the mood and tone of different areas of the set. Warm, inviting colors may be used in communal living spaces, while cooler, harsher tones might be employed in competition areas to heighten the sense of challenge.

The set is also designed with the audience in mind. It needs to be visually engaging and distinct, helping to create a brand identity for the show. Viewers often form a connection with the setting, as it becomes a familiar and integral part of their viewing experience. The design should therefore be memorable and conducive to creating iconic moments that resonate with the audience.

Safety is a paramount concern, especially in shows that involve physical challenges. The design must ensure that all activities are safe for participants, with emergency protocols and medical assistance readily available. This concern extends to psychological safety as well, with spaces like confessionals providing a private outlet for participants to express emotions and stress.

In conclusion, setting the stage for a reality TV show is a complex and creative process that plays a pivotal role in the success of the series. The environment is carefully crafted to enhance the narrative, challenge the contestants, and captivate the audience. It's a balance of aesthetics, functionality, and psychology, creating a world that transforms ordinary people into characters in an extraordinary story. This stage, though silent, speaks volumes, setting the tone for the drama, competition, and human stories that unfold within its confines.

Chapter 5: The Host's Role: Guiding the Narrative

The host of a reality TV show is much more than a presenter or a moderator; they are the vital link between the contestants, the narrative, and the audience. This chapter delves into the multifaceted role of the host, exploring how they guide the narrative, shape viewer perceptions, and become the face of the show.

At the core of the host's role is the ability to narrate the story of the show. They provide context, explain rules, and offer commentary that helps viewers understand and engage with the unfolding events. A skilled host can make complex game mechanics accessible and inject excitement into the proceedings. They are the storytellers who weave the disparate threads of the show into a cohesive narrative.

The host also serves as a mediator and a guide for the contestants. In competitive reality shows, they may oversee challenges, announce results, and mediate disputes. Their presence can be both reassuring and authoritative, providing structure and order within the often chaotic environment of the show. In this role, the host needs to be empathetic yet firm, able to connect with the contestants while maintaining the integrity of the game.

One of the host's most critical roles is to represent the audience's perspective. They ask questions that viewers might have, challenge contestants on their decisions, and express emotions that resonate with the audience. A good host acts as the viewer's surrogate, directly engaging with the show's events and participants. This connection is crucial in maintaining viewer engagement and loyalty.

In addition to their on-screen roles, hosts often become the public face of the show, involved in promotional activities and media appearances. They embody the show's brand and play a key role in its marketing and public perception. A charismatic and popular host can significantly boost a show's appeal, drawing in viewers and keeping them hooked.

The host's influence extends to the production aspects as well. Experienced hosts often contribute to the creative process, offering insights on how to improve the show's format and interaction with contestants. Their on-the-ground experience provides valuable feedback for producers and writers, helping to refine the show's content and delivery.

Another aspect of the host's role is to maintain the ethical standards of the show. They need to ensure that the contestants are treated fairly and that the show's rules are upheld. In situations where contestants face emotional or physical challenges, the host can provide support and intervene if necessary. This role is crucial in maintaining the integrity of the show and ensuring the well-being of its participants.

In conclusion, the host of a reality TV show is a linchpin in its success. They guide the narrative, connect with both contestants and viewers, and embody the spirit of the show. A great host can elevate a reality TV show from merely entertaining to truly memorable, creating a rapport with the audience that lasts long after the season ends. Their role is a delicate balance of presenter, guide, mediator, and ambassador, essential in bringing the drama, excitement, and emotion of the show to life.

Chapter 6: Behind the Lens: The Filming Process

The filming process of a reality TV show is a complex and dynamic operation that captures the essence of real-life drama and action. This chapter provides a behind-the-scenes look at the intricacies of filming a reality show, revealing how the production team works tirelessly to create a seamless and engaging viewer experience.

At the heart of the filming process is the camera crew, who are tasked with capturing the unscripted moments that define reality TV. This requires a high level of skill and flexibility, as they must be able to adapt to spontaneous events and unpredictable contestant behavior. Camera operators often work in challenging conditions, particularly in shows set in remote or confined locations. They must be unobtrusive yet ever-present, ensuring that key moments are captured without influencing the action.

Sound recording is another critical aspect of the filming process. High-quality audio is essential for reality TV, as it captures not just the dialogue but also the subtleties of human emotion and interaction. Sound technicians use a combination of boom microphones, lavaliers, and ambient recording devices to ensure that every whisper, laugh, and argument is clearly heard.

Lighting plays a dual role in the filming process. It must be functional, providing enough light for the cameras to capture clear footage, but it also needs to be aesthetically pleasing, enhancing the visual appeal of the show. In outdoor shows, lighting technicians must contend with changing weather and daylight conditions, while indoor shows require a carefully planned lighting setup that complements the set design.

The use of multiple cameras is a hallmark of reality TV filming. This setup allows for capturing events from various angles, ensuring that the audience doesn't miss any part of the action. In shows like 'Big Brother', where constant surveillance is a key feature, cameras are strategically placed throughout the set to provide 360-degree coverage.

One of the biggest challenges in filming reality TV is the sheer volume of footage generated. Shows that film around the clock can accumulate hundreds of hours of footage, all of which needs to be reviewed, sorted, and edited. This task falls to the production team, who work tirelessly behind the scenes to distill the footage into coherent and engaging episodes.

The director plays a pivotal role in the filming process. They are responsible for overseeing the entire operation, from camera work to contestant interactions. The director must have a clear vision of how each scene fits into the overall narrative of the show and must be able to make quick decisions to capture the most compelling content.

Post-production is a vital part of the filming process. It involves not just editing the footage, but also adding music, sound effects, and visual effects. This stage is where the raw material is transformed into a polished final product. Editors play a crucial role in shaping the narrative, deciding which scenes make it to the final cut and how they are presented.

In conclusion, the filming process of a reality TV show is a multifaceted and labor-intensive operation. It requires a skilled and dedicated team working in unison to capture the unpredictability and drama of real life. From camera operators to sound technicians, lighting experts to editors, each member of the team contributes to creating a captivating and authentic viewer experience. This behind-the-scenes work is as essential to the success of a reality TV show as the on-screen content, turning everyday moments into unforgettable television.

Chapter 7: Crafting Stories: The Power of Editing

Editing is where the raw, unscripted footage of a reality TV show is transformed into a compelling narrative. This chapter focuses on the pivotal role of editing in shaping the story, character arcs, and overall tone of a reality show, highlighting how this process is integral to the success and appeal of the genre.

The primary task of editing in reality TV is to construct a coherent and engaging narrative from hours of disparate footage. This involves selecting key moments that advance the story, create drama, or provide insight into the contestants' personalities and strategies. Editors work like alchemists, turning the mundane into the extraordinary, the chaotic into the coherent. They decide which relationships to focus on, which conflicts to highlight, and which characters to bring to the forefront.

Character development is a crucial aspect of the editing process. Through careful selection and juxtaposition of scenes, editors can craft distinct personalities and story arcs for the contestants. This might involve highlighting certain reactions, confessionals, or interactions that define a contestant's role in the show – be it the antagonist, the comic relief, or the underdog. This character shaping is vital in creating emotional connections between the contestants and the audience.

The pacing of the show is also determined during the editing process. Editors must strike a balance between developing slow-burning narratives and maintaining a rhythm that keeps the audience engaged. This involves deciding when to introduce certain plot points, how long to linger on a moment of tension, and when to provide comedic or emotional relief. The pacing is critical in ensuring that the show remains dynamic and captivating throughout its run.

Another key element in the editing process is the use of music and sound effects. Music can significantly enhance the emotional impact of a scene, whether it's ramping up the tension during a challenge or underscoring a poignant moment between contestants. Sound effects can also be used to heighten reality, adding drama to the contestants' actions and reactions.

Editing also involves a degree of ethical responsibility. Editors must be mindful of how they portray the contestants, ensuring that their editing choices do not misrepresent or unfairly portray individuals. This ethical dimension is crucial in maintaining the integrity of the show and respecting the dignity of those involved.

The visual style of the show is also established during editing. This includes the use of graphics, special effects, and color grading to create a distinctive look and feel. Visual elements can be used to reinforce the show's brand, highlight important information, or simply add an aesthetic appeal. Continuity is another important consideration. Editors must ensure that the sequence of events makes sense and that there are no glaring inconsistencies that could distract or confuse the audience. This is particularly challenging in reality TV, where events are not scripted and can unfold in unpredictable ways.

In conclusion, editing is an art form that is essential to the crafting of a reality TV show. It involves not just cutting and splicing footage, but also shaping narratives, building characters, and creating an emotional resonance with the audience. The power of editing lies in its ability to turn raw reality into a compelling story, making it a fundamental component of the reality TV production process. Through careful and creative editing, the true magic of reality TV comes to life, captivating viewers and keeping them invested in the unfolding drama of real lives.

Chapter 8: Soundscapes: Music and Sound Design

The soundscape of a reality TV show plays a crucial role in shaping the viewer's experience, providing emotional depth and enhancing the narrative. This chapter delves into the intricacies of music selection and sound design in reality TV, exploring how these auditory elements are integral to creating atmosphere, tension, and engagement in the genre.

Music is a powerful tool in reality TV production, used to underscore the emotional tone of a scene. A carefully chosen soundtrack can amplify suspense, joy, sadness, or triumph, guiding the audience's emotional response to the on-screen events. Composers and music supervisors work to create or select music that complements the show's theme and mood. For instance, a tense elimination round might be accompanied by a dramatic, suspenseful score, while a moment of victory could be heightened with uplifting, triumphant music.

The role of music goes beyond just background scoring; it can also be used as a narrative device. Certain themes or motifs may be associated with specific characters or situations, creating a sense of continuity and familiarity for the audience. This thematic use of music helps in building character arcs and reinforcing storylines, subtly influencing the viewer's perception and understanding of the unfolding events.

Sound design in reality TV also involves the skillful manipulation of ambient sounds and sound effects. The sound team works to capture and enhance the natural sounds of the show's environment, whether it's the rustling of leaves in a survival show or the bustling sounds of a cooking competition. These ambient sounds help to create a sense of place and authenticity, immersing the viewer in the show's world.

In addition to natural sounds, sound effects are often used to emphasize certain actions or moments. These can range from subtle cues, like the sound of a timer ticking during a challenge, to more overt effects used for comedic or dramatic emphasis. Sound effects play a crucial role in shaping the show's tone and can be instrumental in creating memorable moments.

The art of mixing and editing sound is also vital. The sound team must balance dialogue, music, and ambient sounds to ensure clarity and impact. The mix needs to be dynamic, allowing for shifts in focus between the spoken word, music, and environmental sounds. This balance is key to maintaining an engaging and coherent auditory experience for the viewer.
Dialogue editing is another important aspect of sound design. In reality TV, where multiple microphones capture overlapping conversations, the clarity of dialogue is essential. Editors work to ensure that key conversations are audible and comprehensible, selecting the best takes and reducing background noise. This process is crucial in conveying the contestants' thoughts, strategies, and emotions to the audience.

In conclusion, the soundscape of a reality TV show is a meticulously crafted element that significantly enhances the viewing experience. Music and sound design work in tandem to create atmosphere, underscore emotion, and reinforce the narrative. They play a fundamental role in immersing the audience in the show's world, accentuating the drama, and connecting viewers emotionally to the events on screen. Through the strategic use of music, ambient sounds, and sound effects, reality TV shows transform from mere visual experiences into rich, multi-sensory journeys.

Chapter 9: Engaging the Audience: Marketing Strategies

The success of a reality TV show is not just measured by its content and production values, but also by its ability to engage and captivate an audience. This chapter explores the diverse and innovative marketing strategies employed in reality TV to attract, retain, and interact with viewers, underscoring the importance of marketing in the genre's popularity and longevity.

A key element of marketing a reality TV show is creating a strong brand identity. This involves crafting a unique and memorable name, logo, and visual style that resonates with the target audience. The brand identity should reflect the essence of the show – its tone, content, and appeal – making it instantly recognizable and distinguishable in a crowded media landscape.

Building anticipation before the show's launch is crucial. This is often achieved through teaser campaigns that give audiences a glimpse of what to expect without revealing too much. These teasers can be in the form of short clips, posters, or social media posts, designed to generate curiosity and excitement. The goal is to create a buzz around the show, encouraging viewers to tune in for the premiere.

Social media plays a pivotal role in the marketing of reality TV shows. Platforms like Instagram, Twitter, and Facebook are used not just for promotion, but also for creating a community around the show. Social media allows for direct interaction with viewers, offering behind-the-scenes content, live Q&A sessions with contestants, and real-time discussions. These interactions help in building a loyal fan base and keeping the audience engaged throughout the season.

Another effective marketing strategy is the use of cross-promotion and partnerships. This can involve collaborations with brands, celebrities, or other media properties that share a similar target audience. These partnerships can take various forms, from product placements within the show to co-branded merchandise and events. Cross-promotion helps in reaching a wider audience and can add an extra layer of interest and credibility to the show.

Viewer engagement is also enhanced through interactive elements. Many reality TV shows incorporate voting mechanisms, allowing viewers to influence the outcome of the show. This not only increases engagement but also gives viewers a sense of ownership and involvement in the show's narrative. Online polls, quizzes, and contests related to the show are other ways to keep the audience actively involved and invested.

Public relations and media coverage are essential components of a reality TV show's marketing strategy. This includes securing coverage in entertainment news, arranging interviews with contestants and hosts, and leveraging events like premieres and finales to generate media buzz. Positive media coverage can significantly boost a show's profile and attract new viewers.

In conclusion, marketing is a critical aspect of the reality TV production process. It involves a combination of branding, anticipation building, social media engagement, cross-promotion, interactive elements, and media relations. These strategies work together to create a compelling narrative around the show, drawing viewers in and keeping them engaged season after season. Through innovative and targeted marketing, reality TV shows can transcend their on-screen presence, becoming cultural phenomena that captivate audiences worldwide.

Chapter 10: The Psychology of Reality TV

The allure of reality TV lies not just in its entertainment value, but also in its psychological appeal. This chapter delves into the psychological aspects that make reality TV a unique and captivating genre, exploring the reasons behind its widespread popularity and the impact it has on both viewers and participants.

At the core of reality TV's appeal is its portrayal of real people facing real situations. This authenticity allows viewers to relate to the participants, creating a sense of connection and empathy. Viewers often see aspects of themselves in the contestants, which can lead to a more invested and emotional viewing experience. This relatability is a key factor in the genre's appeal, as it blurs the line between television and reality, making the drama more impactful.

Another psychological aspect of reality TV is the concept of voyeurism. There is an inherent fascination in observing others, particularly in situations that are unusual or challenging. Reality TV taps into this voyeuristic desire, offering a window into the lives and experiences of others. This can be particularly compelling in shows where participants are placed in extreme or unique environments, as it provides a glimpse into experiences that are far removed from the viewer's everyday life.

The competitive nature of many reality shows also plays into basic human psychology. Competition is a fundamental aspect of human behavior, and watching others compete can be both thrilling and engaging. This is evident in shows where participants are pitted against each other, whether in physical challenges, social games, or talent competitions. The competitive element adds a layer of suspense and excitement, as viewers become invested in the outcome and root for their favorite contestants.

Reality TV also provides a platform for social comparison. Viewers often compare themselves to the participants, in terms of behavior, appearance, skills, and decisions. This comparison can be both positive and negative, as it can lead to feelings of superiority, inspiration, or inadequacy. The social comparison aspect is heightened in reality TV due to its unscripted nature, as it presents real people with all their flaws and strengths.

The impact of reality TV on the participants is another psychological aspect. Being on a reality show can be a highly intense and emotional experience. Participants are often under constant scrutiny, both from their fellow contestants and the viewing public. This can lead to increased stress, anxiety, and in some cases, a distortion of reality. The psychological impact can be lasting, affecting participants' lives long after the show has ended.

The concept of fame and its psychological effects is also prevalent in reality TV. Many participants enter these shows with the hope of gaining fame and recognition. This pursuit of fame can influence their behavior on the show, often leading to exaggerated or strategic actions. The sudden rise to fame that reality TV can provide also has psychological ramifications, as participants must navigate the complexities of public scrutiny and celebrity.

In conclusion, the psychology of reality TV is multifaceted, encompassing the viewer's experience as well as the participant's. The genre's appeal lies in its authenticity, voyeurism, competitive nature, and social comparison aspects. For participants, the psychological impact includes dealing with stress, the pursuit of fame, and the aftermath of public exposure. Understanding these psychological elements is crucial in comprehending the enduring popularity and influence of reality TV, as it continues to be a significant part of contemporary culture and entertainment.

Chapter 11: Drama by Design: Conflict and Resolution

Conflict is the lifeblood of reality TV, driving narratives and keeping audiences engaged. This chapter examines how conflict is intentionally designed and managed in reality TV shows, highlighting the techniques used to create tension and the strategies employed to resolve disputes, ensuring a dynamic yet coherent viewing experience.

The design of conflict in reality TV often starts with the show's format and rules. By setting up competitions, challenges, and tasks that have high stakes, producers create a natural breeding ground for conflict. These situations place contestants under pressure, testing their skills, patience, and interpersonal dynamics. The competition for a prize or title, coupled with the fear of elimination, can lead to rivalries and confrontations, which are central to the drama of the show.

Casting plays a crucial role in designing conflict. Producers often select a diverse group of contestants with differing backgrounds, opinions, and personalities. This diversity is not just about representation; it's a strategic choice to ensure a mix of conflicting viewpoints and potential clashes. For instance, pairing an outspoken, aggressive contestant with a more reserved, peace-loving one can create an interesting dynamic that leads to compelling television.

The environment and living conditions are also used as tools to design conflict. In a show like 'Big Brother', where contestants live together in close quarters, the lack of privacy and personal space can lead to friction. Similarly, in survival-based shows, harsh conditions and limited resources can exacerbate tensions among participants. The environment is thus manipulated to heighten emotions and provoke interactions that might not occur under normal circumstances.

Producers and editors use storytelling techniques to amplify and shape conflicts. Through selective editing, they can highlight certain aspects of a conflict, giving it more prominence and shaping the audience's perception of the participants involved. Narration and confessionals are also used to provide context to conflicts, offering insight into the contestants' thoughts and motivations.

While conflict is essential to reality TV, so is its resolution. Resolution provides a narrative closure, ensuring that the conflict does not overshadow the entire show. It can come in the form of a contestant's elimination, a reconciliation between participants, or an intervention by the host. The resolution is important not just for narrative purposes, but also for maintaining a level of harmony and ensuring the show remains enjoyable to watch.

Ethical considerations are crucial when designing conflict. While drama is key to the show's success, it should not come at the cost of a participant's well-being. Producers must ensure that conflicts do not escalate to harmful levels and that participants have access to support if needed. The portrayal of conflict must also be balanced and fair, avoiding the demonization or unfair treatment of any contestant.

In conclusion, conflict in reality TV is a carefully orchestrated element that adds excitement and drama to the show. It is designed through the show's format, casting, environment, and storytelling techniques. However, it is balanced with resolution to provide narrative structure and maintain viewer engagement. Ethical considerations are paramount to ensure that while conflict is a central aspect of the show, it does not compromise the integrity of the participants or the program. Through this delicate balance of conflict and resolution, reality TV captivates audiences, providing a mix of drama, tension, and entertainment.

Chapter 12: Ethics in Reality TV Production

The production of reality TV involves a myriad of ethical considerations, ranging from the treatment of participants to the portrayal of real-life events. This chapter delves into the ethical challenges and responsibilities inherent in reality TV production, underscoring the importance of maintaining integrity and respect throughout the creative process.

One of the primary ethical concerns in reality TV is the welfare of the participants. Producers and networks have a responsibility to ensure that participants are not placed in harmful situations, physically or psychologically. This includes proper vetting for physical challenges, providing psychological support, and ensuring a safe living environment. The intense scrutiny and pressure that come with being on a reality show can have significant impacts on participants' mental health, making ongoing support and aftercare crucial.

Consent and transparency are also key ethical issues. Participants should be fully informed about the nature of the show, the extent of filming, and how they might be portrayed. This includes understanding the editing process and how it can potentially alter the context of their actions and words. Informed consent is not a one-time process but an ongoing conversation throughout the show's production.

The portrayal of reality is another ethical consideration. While editing is essential for crafting a compelling narrative, it should not distort the truth or misrepresent events. Selective editing can create misleading narratives or false impressions of participants, raising questions about fairness and authenticity. Ethical editing practices are essential to maintain the integrity of the show and respect for those involved.

Respecting the privacy and dignity of participants is a further ethical concern. Even in a genre built on surveillance and exposure, there must be limits to how far the cameras intrude into participants' lives. This includes respecting moments of vulnerability and ensuring that participants are not exploited for sensationalist content.

The representation of diversity and avoidance of stereotyping are also important. Reality TV should strive to present a diverse range of participants and avoid reinforcing harmful stereotypes. This involves thoughtful casting and a commitment to portraying individuals in a multifaceted and respectful manner.

Dealing with conflict and sensitive situations ethically is also crucial. While conflict is a staple of reality TV, it should be handled in a way that does not encourage harmful behavior or glorify toxicity. Interventions should be made when conflicts escalate to unhealthy levels, and the portrayal of such conflicts should be handled sensitively.

Lastly, the impact of reality TV on broader societal norms and values should be considered. Producers and networks should be aware of the influence their content can have on public perceptions and behavior. This responsibility involves considering the messages that the show sends about issues such as relationships, success, and personal values.

In conclusion, ethics in reality TV production is a complex and critical aspect that requires careful consideration and responsible decision-making. From ensuring the welfare and respectful treatment of participants to maintaining honesty and integrity in the portrayal of reality, ethical practices are fundamental. They not only protect those involved in the show but also contribute to the credibility and sustainability of the reality TV genre as a whole. Through ethical production practices, reality TV can continue to entertain and engage audiences without compromising its integrity or social responsibility.

Chapter 13: Reality vs. Fiction: The Viewer's Dilemma

The blurred lines between reality and fiction in reality TV create a unique dilemma for viewers. This chapter explores the complexities of this viewer experience, examining how reality TV straddles the realms of authenticity and dramatization, and the impact this has on audience perception and engagement.

At the heart of the viewer's dilemma is the question of authenticity. Reality TV, by its very nature, purports to show real people in real situations. However, the involvement of production elements like editing, scripting scenarios, and casting for dramatic effect, can lead to doubts about the genuineness of what is being portrayed. Viewers are often left wondering how much of the show is an accurate reflection of reality and how much is embellished for entertainment.

This dilemma is further complicated by the role of participants. Unlike actors in scripted shows, reality TV stars are not playing characters but are supposed to be themselves. Yet, the awareness of being filmed and the desire to portray a certain image or achieve specific outcomes can lead to behavior that is more performative than genuine. This performative aspect raises questions about the authenticity of the participants' actions and emotions.

The editing process also plays a significant role in this dilemma. The way footage is cut, rearranged, and presented can drastically alter the context of events and interactions. This power of editing shapes narratives and can create heroes, villains, or love stories where the raw footage might tell a different story. It challenges viewers to discern how much of the drama and narrative arcs are organic and how much are constructs of the editing room.

Another aspect of the dilemma is the impact of reality TV on societal perceptions and norms. Shows that depict extreme behavior, conflict, or stereotypical portrayals can influence viewers' understanding of social interactions and human behavior. This influence can be problematic, especially if it reinforces negative stereotypes or unrealistic expectations about relationships, success, and personal values.

Despite these issues, the allure of reality TV lies in its unscripted nature and the spontaneity of its participants. The genre offers a form of entertainment that feels more relatable and less predictable than scripted television. It provides a window into different lifestyles and experiences, and at times, can be a platform for exploring social issues, personal struggles, and human triumphs.

Viewers often navigate this dilemma by engaging with reality TV on multiple levels. Some watch it for pure entertainment, enjoying the dramatic narratives while acknowledging the manipulations of production. Others engage more critically, questioning the portrayal of events and the behavior of participants. Social media and online forums have become platforms for viewers to discuss and dissect shows, blurring the line between consuming and critiquing.

In conclusion, the dilemma of reality versus fiction in reality TV is a central aspect of its appeal and criticism. It challenges viewers to question the authenticity of what they watch, while also providing a form of entertainment that is engaging and relatable. This complexity is what makes reality TV a unique and enduring genre, continually captivating audiences who are drawn to the drama of real life, however constructed it may be.

Chapter 14: The Evolution of Reality TV Genres

Reality TV has undergone significant evolution since its inception, diversifying into various genres and sub-genres that cater to a wide range of audiences. This chapter explores the trajectory of this evolution, highlighting how changes in societal interests, technological advancements, and creative innovation have shaped the landscape of reality TV.

The early days of reality TV were marked by documentary-style programs that focused on observing real-life situations. Shows like 'Candid Camera' and 'An American Family' paved the way, offering viewers a glimpse into the lives and experiences of others. These shows were primarily observational, with minimal intervention from producers or hosts.

As the genre gained popularity, a new wave of reality TV emerged, focusing on competition and survival. Shows like 'Survivor' and 'Big Brother' introduced the concept of placing participants in challenging environments or competitive scenarios. These shows added elements of strategy, alliance-building, and physical endurance, creating a more dynamic and suspenseful viewing experience.

The rise of talent-based reality shows marked another significant evolution in the genre. Programs like 'American Idol' and 'Dancing with the Stars' shifted the focus to showcasing and discovering new talent. These shows combined the appeal of competition with the excitement of live performances, creating platforms for aspiring artists to gain recognition.

Reality TV also expanded into lifestyle and self-improvement genres. Shows like 'The Biggest Loser' and 'Queer Eye' focused on personal transformations, whether in terms of physical health, fashion, or home renovation. These shows often had an inspirational tone, aiming to motivate and uplift both participants and viewers.

Dating and relationship-themed reality shows became a genre in their own right. From 'The Bachelor' to 'Married at First Sight', these shows explore the complexities of relationships and the drama of romantic entanglements. They often combine elements of competition with soap opera-style narratives, creating emotionally charged and often controversial content.

Another significant evolution in reality TV is the integration of social media and interactive elements. With the rise of digital platforms, shows have started to incorporate viewer participation through online voting, social media challenges, and interactive apps. This evolution has transformed viewers from passive observers to active participants, influencing the outcomes of shows and engaging with content on multiple levels.

Reality TV has also seen a trend towards niche and specialized content. This includes shows focused on specific professions, hobbies, or lifestyles, catering to audiences with particular interests. From cooking competitions to home renovation challenges, these shows provide in-depth and specialized content that appeals to specific segments of viewers.

In conclusion, the evolution of reality TV genres reflects the changing tastes and interests of audiences, as well as advancements in technology and media. From its humble beginnings as observational documentaries to its current status as a diverse and dynamic entertainment genre, reality TV has continuously adapted and innovated. This evolution has not only expanded the scope and reach of reality TV but has also cemented its place as a significant and influential part of popular culture.

Chapter 15: Social Dynamics: Alliances and Rivalries

In the intricate tapestry of reality TV, the social dynamics of alliances and rivalries play a pivotal role. This chapter delves into how these relationships are formed, evolved, and displayed on screen, and their impact on both the narrative of the show and the viewer experience.

Alliances in reality TV are often formed out of necessity or strategy. In competitive formats, where contestants are vying for a prize or seeking to avoid elimination, alliances can provide a tactical advantage. Participants may align based on shared interests, strengths, or even out of convenience. These alliances are dynamic and can shift as the game progresses, adding an element of unpredictability and intrigue to the show.

The formation of alliances also reveals much about human behavior and social psychology. They often require trust, negotiation, and sometimes betrayal, mirroring the complexities of real-life relationships. Alliances can be straightforward or fraught with deception and duplicity, reflecting the diverse nature of human interactions. Viewers often become invested in these alliances, rooting for them to succeed or fail, which enhances engagement with the show.

Rivalries, on the other hand, add a different flavor to the social dynamics of reality TV. They can arise from competition, personality clashes, or conflicts over strategy. Rivalries often bring drama and tension to the show, creating compelling narratives that captivate audiences. They can be overt and confrontational or subtle and passive-aggressive, but always add an element of excitement to the show.

The portrayal of alliances and rivalries is crucial in how the show is received by the audience. Editing plays a significant role in this portrayal, highlighting certain aspects of these relationships to enhance the drama. The way these dynamics are presented can influence viewer perceptions, making certain contestants heroes, villains, or underdogs.

Alliances and rivalries also serve as a microcosm of societal interactions. They can highlight issues such as teamwork, leadership, trust, and conflict resolution. In some cases, they can also bring to light deeper societal issues like prejudice, stereotyping, and the abuse of power. This can make reality TV a platform for exploring and discussing broader social themes.
The impact of these social dynamics extends beyond the show. Participants, often thrown into intense and emotional environments, can form lasting relationships or enduring conflicts. The experience of forming alliances and engaging in rivalries can have a profound impact on their personal growth and understanding of social interactions.

In conclusion, alliances and rivalries are central to the fabric of reality TV. They provide strategic depth, emotional complexity, and dramatic tension to the shows. These dynamics not only enhance the entertainment value of the genre but also offer insights into human behavior and social relationships. Through the lens of alliances and rivalries, reality TV reflects and amplifies the drama of real-life social interactions, making it a captivating and often revealing genre.

Chapter 16: The Digital Frontier: Social Media Integration

The integration of social media into reality TV represents a significant shift in how these shows are produced, consumed, and engaged with. This chapter explores the multifaceted impact of social media on reality TV, highlighting how it has transformed audience interaction, participant exposure, and the overall narrative of the genre.

Social media has become an essential tool for reality TV shows, serving as a platform for promotion, engagement, and extension of the show's narrative. Platforms like Twitter, Instagram, and Facebook allow shows to reach audiences beyond the confines of traditional broadcast times. They offer sneak peeks, behind-the-scenes content, and additional insights into the participants' lives and personalities, creating a more immersive and engaging viewer experience.

Audience interaction is one of the key areas where social media integration has made a profound impact. Viewers can share their opinions, predictions, and reactions in real-time, creating a communal viewing experience even when watching alone. This instant feedback loop also provides valuable insights for producers, who can gauge audience sentiments and adjust future content accordingly.

Social media has also changed the game for participants of reality shows. Contestants can leverage these platforms to build their personal brand, connect with fans, and extend their fame beyond the show. However, this exposure also comes with challenges, such as dealing with public scrutiny, criticism, and the pressure to maintain a certain image online.

Another significant impact of social media is on the narrative structure of reality TV. Audience reactions and interactions on social media can influence the direction of the show. Voting polls, hashtag campaigns, and online discussions can sway public opinion and potentially affect the outcomes of the show, making the audience active participants in the narrative.

Social media has also given rise to ancillary content that complements the main show. This includes spin-off mini-series, live Q&A sessions with participants, and interactive online games. These extensions enrich the show's universe and offer additional touch points for audience engagement. Moreover, the immediacy and reach of social media have led to a more dynamic relationship between reality TV shows and their audiences. In the past, viewer feedback was limited to letters and occasional phone surveys. Now, producers and participants can receive instant reactions to episodes, decisions, and characters. This immediacy can be a double-edged sword; it allows for real-time adjustments to content based on viewer preferences, but it also exposes shows and participants to instant, widespread criticism.

The integration of social media has also led to the phenomenon of second-screen viewing. Viewers often use social media platforms on their smartphones or tablets to comment on episodes as they air live. This simultaneous engagement creates a multi-dimensional experience, where the act of watching is just as interactive as the content itself. It fosters a sense of community among viewers, as they share reactions, memes, and commentary in real-time.

In addition to enhancing viewer engagement, social media has transformed participants of reality TV into instant celebrities. Contestants can build significant online followings during and after the show, which they can leverage for personal branding, endorsements, and continued public presence. This instant fame, however, comes with its challenges, as participants must navigate the complex world of online publicity and manage their public personas.

For producers, social media has become a vital tool for gauging the success and reach of their shows. Trends, hashtags, and viewer engagement metrics provide valuable data that can inform future production decisions. This data-driven approach helps in tailoring content to audience preferences, potentially increasing viewership and loyalty to the show.

However, the influence of social media on narrative structure raises questions about authenticity and spontaneity. As producers potentially adjust content based on social media feedback, there is a risk of the show losing its unscripted nature. This balancing act between audience engagement and maintaining the integrity of the show is a nuanced challenge in the modern landscape of reality TV.

In conclusion, social media integration has significantly impacted the narrative structure, viewer engagement, and participant experience in reality TV. It has opened up new avenues for interaction, community building, and audience influence, changing the way these shows are consumed and perceived. As reality TV continues to evolve with digital trends, the relationship between the show, its participants, and the audience will likely continue to grow more intertwined, offering new possibilities and challenges for this dynamic genre.

Chapter 17: Viewer Interaction: Beyond the Screen

The evolution of reality TV has been significantly influenced by the ways in which viewers interact with the content beyond the traditional TV screen. This chapter delves into the diverse forms of viewer interaction that have become integral to the reality TV experience, examining how these interactions deepen engagement, influence the show's direction, and create a more participatory form of entertainment.

One of the most direct forms of viewer interaction in reality TV is through voting. Many shows incorporate audience votes to decide outcomes such as eliminations or winners. This involvement gives viewers a sense of agency, as they can directly impact the narrative and fate of the contestants. It also increases investment in the show, as viewers feel more connected to the outcomes when they have a hand in shaping them.

Online forums and social media platforms have become virtual spaces where viewers dissect episodes, share theories, and discuss contestants' strategies. These discussions extend the life of each episode beyond its airtime, keeping viewers engaged with the show throughout the week. Fan theories and discussions can sometimes influence the perception of contestants and the narrative, as producers monitor these conversations and gain insights into the audience's views.

Interactive apps and websites associated with reality TV shows offer additional content such as quizzes, games, and exclusive interviews. These platforms not only provide entertainment but also enhance the viewer's knowledge and connection to the show. They often include features that allow viewers to track contestants' progress, predict outcomes, and even participate in fantasy leagues. Viewer interaction also extends to live events and meet-and-greets. These events, whether virtual or in-person, allow fans to interact with contestants and hosts, adding a layer of reality to the TV experience. They provide an opportunity for fans to engage with the show on a more personal level, fostering a sense of community among viewers and participants.

The feedback loop created by viewer interaction is also valuable for producers and networks. Audience reactions, whether through social media, ratings, or direct feedback, provide real-time data that can influence future content. This responsiveness to viewer preferences can help in maintaining the show's relevance and appeal.

However, this level of interaction also raises challenges. The line between engagement and invasion of privacy can become blurred, especially when viewers take to social media to express unsolicited opinions about contestants. The mental health and well-being of contestants can be impacted by negative feedback and cyberbullying. Therefore, responsible engagement practices need to be encouraged, and support systems should be in place for participants dealing with public scrutiny.

In conclusion, viewer interaction in reality TV has transformed the genre into a more interactive and engaging form of entertainment. It allows viewers to extend their experience beyond the screen, participating in and influencing the world of the show. This interactivity enhances the investment and enjoyment of the audience but also requires careful management to ensure a positive and respectful environment for both viewers and participants. Through these interactive elements, reality TV continues to evolve, adapting to the changing media landscape and viewer expectations.

Chapter 18: The Global Impact of Reality TV

The influence of reality TV extends far beyond individual national borders, having a profound global impact. This chapter explores how reality TV has become a significant cultural phenomenon worldwide, influencing entertainment, societal norms, and even international relations.

Reality TV shows have transcended their countries of origin, captivating global audiences. Formats like 'Survivor', 'Big Brother', and 'The Apprentice' have been adapted in numerous countries, each version reflecting its local culture and societal values. This global proliferation demonstrates the universal appeal of the genre's themes, such as competition, survival, and human interaction.

The international success of these shows has led to cross-cultural exchanges and increased global awareness. Viewers are exposed to different cultures, lifestyles, and perspectives, broadening their understanding and appreciation of diversity. Shows that focus on travel or cultural challenges, like 'The Amazing Race', specifically highlight this aspect, showcasing the customs, landscapes, and people of different countries.

Reality TV has also influenced global entertainment industries. It has created a model for low-cost, high-impact programming that can yield significant returns. This model is particularly appealing in markets with limited production budgets. Additionally, the success of reality TV has prompted international collaborations, with production companies across different countries partnering to create new content.

The genre has had a notable impact on global advertising and marketing strategies. Brands have recognized the power of reality TV to reach wide and diverse audiences. Product placements, sponsorships, and branded content within these shows have become common, offering companies a unique way to market their products and services on a global scale.

However, the global impact of reality TV is not without its controversies. The genre has been criticized for promoting materialism, superficiality, and unrealistic standards of beauty and success. In some cases, it has also been accused of perpetuating stereotypes and cultural insensitivity, especially in shows that involve participants from different cultural backgrounds.

Reality TV's global reach has also spurred discussions about the homogenization of entertainment. There is a concern that the widespread adoption of certain reality TV formats might overshadow local television traditions and narratives, leading to a loss of cultural diversity in programming.

In conclusion, the global impact of reality TV is multifaceted. While it has become a powerful cultural export, influencing entertainment, marketing, and societal norms worldwide, it also raises questions about cultural representation and the effects of globalized media. As reality TV continues to evolve, its ability to adapt to different cultural contexts while maintaining a universal appeal will be crucial in shaping its ongoing global impact and legacy.

Chapter 19: Reality TV and Cultural Representation

Reality TV, with its wide reach and diverse formats, plays a significant role in cultural representation. This chapter examines how reality TV portrays various cultures, identities, and social issues, and the implications of these portrayals for viewers and society at large.

A primary aspect of reality TV is its potential to showcase a broad spectrum of individuals and lifestyles, providing visibility to diverse groups. Shows that feature participants from various ethnic, racial, and social backgrounds can promote understanding and tolerance. When done well, this representation can challenge stereotypes and offer a more nuanced view of different cultures and communities.

However, the portrayal of cultures in reality TV is often a double-edged sword. While these shows can provide a platform for underrepresented groups, they can also perpetuate stereotypes and simplistic narratives. The editing process can sometimes highlight conflicts or behaviors that reinforce negative stereotypes, leading to criticism about the misrepresentation of certain groups.

The inclusion of contestants from diverse backgrounds also raises questions about tokenism versus genuine representation. Shows must navigate the line between including diverse participants for genuine representation and using them merely to tick diversity boxes. Authentic representation involves not only showcasing diverse contestants but also giving them equal narrative space and depth.

Reality TV also has the power to bring social issues to the forefront. Shows that tackle themes like poverty, addiction, or mental health can raise awareness and stimulate discussion. However, it is crucial that these issues are handled sensitively and ethically, without exploiting the participants' struggles for entertainment value.

The global nature of reality TV also contributes to cultural exchange and representation. International formats adapted in different countries often retain the core concept while incorporating local cultural elements. This adaptation can foster a mutual exchange of cultural values and practices, enriching the show and its audience.

The portrayal of gender and sexuality in reality TV is another area with significant cultural implications. Shows that include and positively represent a range of gender identities and sexual orientations can be instrumental in promoting acceptance and understanding. However, these portrayals must avoid clichés and tokenism, striving for authenticity and respect.

Audience reaction and feedback, particularly through social media, play a critical role in shaping the cultural representation in reality TV. Viewer responses can highlight issues of representation and inclusivity, prompting producers to make adjustments in future programming.

In conclusion, reality TV holds considerable power in shaping cultural narratives and representations. While it can be a force for promoting diversity and understanding, it also bears the responsibility of avoiding stereotypes and misrepresentation. As the genre continues to evolve, it is essential that reality TV reflects the complexity and richness of the cultures it represents, contributing positively to societal understanding and cohesion.

Chapter 20: The Legalities of Reality TV Production

The production of reality TV involves navigating a complex landscape of legal considerations. This chapter explores the various legal aspects that producers must contend with, from contracts and rights management to issues of privacy and defamation, highlighting the importance of legal compliance in the creation and distribution of reality TV content.

One of the primary legal considerations in reality TV is the use of contracts. Participants, hosts, and crew members are typically required to sign contracts that outline the terms of their involvement, compensation, and obligations. These contracts often include non-disclosure agreements to prevent leaks of show content and non-disparagement clauses to protect the show's reputation. For participants, contracts might also specify the extent of their participation, the handling of any prize money, and stipulations regarding their behavior on the show.

Rights management is another critical legal aspect. This includes securing the rights to any intellectual property used in the show, such as music, logos, and branded content. Failure to properly manage these rights can lead to costly legal disputes and infringement issues. Additionally, the format rights for shows that are adaptations of foreign formats need to be obtained and managed in accordance with international intellectual property laws.

Privacy concerns are paramount in reality TV production. Although participants consent to being filmed, there are limits to what can be legally and ethically recorded and broadcast. The editing process must respect participants' privacy and dignity, avoiding the portrayal of scenes that could be considered invasive or harmful. Legal issues arise when the line between public interest and an individual's right to privacy is crossed.

Defamation and libel are potential risks in reality TV. The portrayal of participants in a negative light could lead to legal claims if they believe their reputation has been unjustly harmed. Producers must ensure that the content of the show does not defame any individuals, either explicitly or implicitly.

The handling of potentially illegal activities captured during filming is another legal challenge. Producers must decide how to deal with footage that depicts illegal behavior, balancing the show's authenticity with legal responsibilities. This might involve working with legal authorities or editing out certain content.

Compliance with broadcasting standards and regulations is essential. This includes adhering to rules regarding content appropriateness, advertising, and product placements. Different countries have varying regulations, and international shows must navigate these differences to ensure compliance in all broadcast regions.

In conclusion, the legalities of reality TV production are diverse and complex. Producers must carefully navigate contracts, rights management, privacy concerns, defamation risks, legal compliance, and the handling of illegal activities. Adherence to legal standards is not just about avoiding disputes and penalties; it also upholds the integrity of the show and protects the rights and well-being of everyone involved. As reality TV continues to evolve, staying abreast of legal developments and challenges remains crucial for the successful and ethical production of these shows.

Chapter 21: Editing Narratives: Perception vs. Reality

The art of editing in reality TV is a balancing act between crafting compelling narratives and maintaining the authenticity of real-life events. This chapter delves into the nuances of editing in reality TV, exploring how it shapes viewers' perceptions and the ethical considerations involved in balancing storytelling with reality.

Editing is fundamental in transforming hours of raw footage into coherent, engaging episodes. Editors are tasked with selecting moments that advance the narrative, create drama, or provide insight into contestants' personalities and strategies. This process involves decisions about what to include, what to omit, and how to present events. The power of editing can significantly alter viewers' perceptions, turning mundane moments into dramatic scenes, and shaping the audience's opinions of contestants.

The narrative constructed through editing is a key element of a reality TV show's appeal. It involves creating story arcs, building suspense, and developing characters. Editors often use techniques like foreshadowing, flashback, and thematic editing to enhance the storytelling. However, this narrative construction can sometimes lead to a version of events that diverges from the actual occurrences, raising questions about the authenticity of the portrayal.

The portrayal of contestants is a particularly sensitive aspect of editing. The way in which individuals are depicted can have a significant impact on their public image and personal life. 'Villains', 'heroes', and 'comedic characters' are often created through selective editing, which can be misleading or unfair. This aspect of editing raises ethical questions about the responsibility of reality TV producers to present a truthful depiction of events and personalities.

Editing also influences the emotional tone of the show. Music, sound effects, and visual techniques are used to evoke specific emotions in the audience. This emotional manipulation is a powerful tool in engaging viewers but must be used judiciously to avoid misrepresenting the reality of situations.

The concept of 'frankenbiting', where disparate pieces of audio are edited together to create a new narrative, is another controversial aspect of editing. This technique can be used to generate compelling content, but it also risks distorting the truth and misleading the audience.

Viewer awareness of editing techniques has increased, with many audiences now savvy about the realities of reality TV production. This awareness has led to a demand for more authentic and less manipulated content, challenging editors and producers to find new ways to maintain viewer interest without resorting to deceptive practices.

In conclusion, editing narratives in reality TV is a complex interplay of perception and reality. While editing is essential in creating engaging and coherent narratives, it also comes with the responsibility to portray events and personalities truthfully. The challenge for reality TV lies in finding the right balance, crafting compelling stories while respecting the authenticity of the real-life events and individuals they depict. As viewer awareness grows, the pressure to uphold ethical editing practices will likely increase, shaping the future of reality TV production.

Chapter 22: The Role of Producers: Puppeteers of Drama

The producers of reality TV shows are often likened to puppeteers, subtly orchestrating the drama that unfolds on screen. This chapter delves into the multifaceted role of producers in reality TV, examining how they shape content, manage participants, and navigate the fine line between creating compelling television and respecting the authenticity of real-life events.

Producers play a central role in the conception and development of a reality TV show. They are involved in everything from conceptualizing the show's format to selecting the cast and determining the challenges or tasks the participants will face. This initial stage sets the tone for the type of drama and interactions that will occur, making the producer's role crucial in defining the show's direction.

Once filming begins, producers become the architects of drama. They may influence events by introducing surprise elements, altering the environment, or manipulating scenarios to heighten tension and conflict. For instance, in a show like 'Survivor', producers might introduce unexpected twists or merge teams to stir dynamics and create new alliances or rivalries.

Producers also play a significant role in managing the participants. They often interact with contestants to gauge their emotions and thoughts, which can influence how they steer the show. While ensuring that participants are safe and their needs are met, producers also have to encourage them to be engaging and dynamic on screen. This aspect of the role involves a delicate balance between being supportive and pushing contestants to reveal more of themselves.

The ethical considerations in a producer's role cannot be overstated. They must ensure that the competition is fair, the portrayal of participants is balanced, and that the show does not cross the line into exploitation. They are responsible for maintaining a respectful and safe environment, both physically and psychologically, for everyone involved in the production.

Producers also work closely with the editing team to shape the final narrative of the show. They help decide which storylines are highlighted and how the characters are developed through the footage. This stage is crucial in determining how the reality captured by the cameras is transformed into the story that audiences will see.

Viewer engagement is another key area of focus for producers. They need to understand what keeps audiences interested and how to adapt the show to maintain its appeal. This often involves staying attuned to viewer feedback and social media trends, using these insights to make real-time adjustments to the show's content.

In conclusion, the role of producers in reality TV is complex and influential. They are the unseen forces behind the drama and entertainment that define the genre. While they have the power to create captivating television, they also carry the responsibility of doing so ethically and respectfully. As the architects of reality TV drama, producers must navigate the challenges of crafting engaging content while maintaining the integrity of the participants and the authenticity of the show.

Chapter 23: Behind the Scenes: Crew and Logistics

The success of a reality TV show hinges not only on the on-screen talent and producers but also on the often-unseen efforts of the crew and the meticulous planning of logistics. This chapter illuminates the crucial role played by the behind-the-scenes teams in reality TV production, highlighting the complexities of logistics, technical expertise, and teamwork required to bring these shows to life.

The crew of a reality TV show encompasses a wide range of professionals, each specializing in different aspects of production. Camera operators, sound technicians, lighting experts, and production designers work in unison to capture the raw footage essential for the show. Their expertise in dealing with unpredictable conditions and capturing spontaneous moments is vital in creating the authentic feel that reality TV demands.

Sound is a critical component of reality TV, and the role of the sound crew is multifaceted. They must ensure that dialogue is captured clearly, often in challenging environments, and balance this with ambient sounds to create a realistic and engaging audio experience. The sound team's work extends into post-production, where they collaborate with editors to fine-tune the audio for the final cut.

Lighting teams also play a pivotal role, particularly in shows filmed in controlled environments like studios. They create lighting setups that enhance the visual appeal of the set, support the mood of different scenes, and ensure that all action is well-lit and camera-ready.

The production design team is responsible for creating the physical environment of the show, from designing sets that reflect the show's theme to managing props and materials for challenges or tasks. Their work is crucial in establishing the aesthetic and functional aspects of the show's setting. Logistics and coordination are the backbone of reality TV production. This includes managing schedules, securing locations, arranging transportation, and ensuring that all equipment and personnel are in the right place at the right time. The logistical team also handles permits, legal requirements, and local regulations, especially in shows that are filmed across multiple locations or involve travel.

Catering and welfare services are also an integral part of the crew's responsibilities. They ensure that the cast and crew are well-fed and looked after, particularly in remote or challenging filming locations. This support is essential for maintaining morale and energy levels throughout the demanding production schedule.

Safety is paramount in reality TV production, especially in shows that involve physical challenges or extreme environments. Safety officers and medical teams are on hand to assess risks, provide necessary training, and respond to any emergencies. Their presence is vital in ensuring the well-being of everyone involved in the production.

In conclusion, the behind-the-scenes crew and logistics teams are the unsung heroes of reality TV. Their expertise, dedication, and coordination are crucial in transforming concepts into captivating television. From the initial planning stages to the final days of shooting, these professionals work tirelessly, often under challenging conditions, to ensure the smooth execution and success of reality TV shows. Their contributions, though less visible to the audience, are fundamental to the creation of the compelling and dynamic content that defines the genre.

Chapter 24: Contestant Selection: The Audition Process

The audition process is a critical phase in the making of a reality TV show, as it sets the stage for the type of dynamics, drama, and interactions that will unfold. This chapter delves into the intricate process of selecting contestants, highlighting the strategies employed to assemble a diverse, compelling, and suitable cast for various reality TV formats.

The initial step in the audition process often involves a public call for participants. This can be done through social media, advertisements, and casting calls on the show's website. The goal is to attract a wide range of applicants, ensuring diversity in terms of demographics, personalities, and backgrounds. In some cases, casting scouts may also actively search for potential contestants who possess specific qualities or fit certain roles envisioned for the show.

Once applications are received, the screening process begins. This involves reviewing application forms, photos, and any required audition videos. Casting teams look for individuals who stand out in terms of their story, personality, and potential for creating interesting television. They seek a mix of traits, from charisma and confidence to uniqueness and authenticity.

Selected applicants are then usually invited for interviews. These interviews can range from informal conversations to more structured assessments, including psychological evaluations and on-camera tests. The aim is to gauge the applicants' suitability for the show, their ability to handle pressure, and how they might interact with others. Personality tests and background checks are also common to ensure the safety and compatibility of contestants.

For shows that require specific skills or talents, such as cooking or singing competitions, auditions may involve skill demonstrations. These auditions are not only about assessing the level of skill but also how contestants present themselves and their ability to perform under pressure.
The dynamics of the potential cast are a crucial consideration in the selection process. Producers and casting directors envision how different personalities will interact, aiming to create a balance that can lead to interesting alliances, rivalries, and narratives. The selection process, therefore, involves a mix of individual assessments and considerations of group chemistry.

Ethical considerations are paramount throughout the audition process. It is vital to ensure that contestants are treated fairly, that their well-being is considered, and that they are fully aware of what participation in the show entails. This includes being transparent about the challenges they may face and the impact on their personal lives.

In conclusion, the audition process in reality TV is a comprehensive and strategic operation. It involves not just selecting individuals who are compelling on their own but also assembling a group that will collectively create engaging and dynamic television. From initial applications to in-depth interviews and skill assessments, each stage of the process is designed to ensure that the final cast is well-suited to the show's format and objectives. This careful curation of contestants is fundamental to the success of a reality TV show, setting the foundation for the drama, entertainment, and human stories that captivate audiences.

Chapter 25: Reality TV's Influence on Society

Reality TV, with its broad reach and diverse content, has a significant influence on societal norms, values, and behaviors. This chapter examines the multifaceted impact of reality TV on society, exploring both its positive contributions and its potential negative effects.

One of the most noticeable impacts of reality TV is its role in shaping cultural norms and perceptions. Shows that feature diverse casts and tackle various social issues can promote understanding and acceptance of different lifestyles and viewpoints. They can challenge stereotypes and broaden viewers' perspectives by showcasing a wide range of human experiences and backgrounds.

However, reality TV also has the potential to reinforce negative stereotypes and promote unhealthy behaviors. Shows that thrive on conflict, aggression, or sensationalism can normalize these behaviors and attitudes, especially among impressionable audiences. The portrayal of unrealistic lifestyles and standards, often seen in shows about wealth and luxury, can also skew viewers' perceptions of success and happiness.

The genre has influenced societal views on privacy and personal boundaries. With the ubiquity of reality TV, the line between public and private life has become increasingly blurred. This shift can lead to a culture of surveillance and oversharing, where personal experiences are commodified and public scrutiny is normalized.

Reality TV has also contributed to the democratization of celebrity. It has created a pathway for ordinary individuals to achieve fame and influence. This shift has impacted traditional notions of celebrity, making it seem more accessible and attainable. However, it also raises questions about the nature of fame and the transient nature of celebrity in the digital age.

The interactive nature of many reality shows, where viewers vote or comment on participants, has led to increased audience engagement and participation. This interactivity can foster a sense of community and shared experience among viewers. However, it can also lead to negative consequences, such as cyberbullying or intense scrutiny of contestants' lives.

Moreover, reality TV has influenced consumer behavior through product placements and brand partnerships. Viewers are often introduced to products and brands through their integration into reality TV shows, impacting purchasing decisions and consumer trends.

In conclusion, reality TV wields a considerable influence on society. It has the power to shape cultural norms, perceptions, and behaviors, for better or worse. While it can be a force for positive change and representation, it also carries the risk of reinforcing negative stereotypes and promoting unhealthy societal trends. Understanding the impact of reality TV is crucial for viewers, producers, and participants alike, as it continues to be a pervasive and influential element of contemporary culture.

Chapter 26: The Economics of Reality TV

The economic landscape of reality TV is a complex and multifaceted domain, marked by its cost-effectiveness and substantial revenue-generating potential. This chapter delves into the economics behind reality TV, exploring how the genre achieves financial success and the various factors influencing its profitability.

One of the key economic advantages of reality TV is its relatively low production cost compared to scripted television. The absence of paid actors, scriptwriters, and expensive set constructions significantly reduces expenses. Additionally, shooting in real locations, often with handheld cameras, further cuts down on costs. This cost-effectiveness makes reality TV an attractive option for networks and producers, especially in a market saturated with high-budget productions.

The revenue model for reality TV often includes more than just traditional advertising income. Product placements and brand integrations within the shows are lucrative sources of revenue. Brands pay to have their products featured in a way that integrates seamlessly with the show's content, providing them with a captive audience and a subtle marketing approach.

Syndication and format sales also contribute to the economic success of reality TV. Popular shows are often adapted and licensed to different countries, creating additional revenue streams. The flexibility of reality TV formats to be tailored to different cultures and languages makes them appealing for international adaptations.

Audience engagement is a significant driver of economic value in reality TV. Engaged audiences not only boost ratings but also contribute to the show's social media presence and online buzz. This engagement can be monetized through merchandise sales, live events, and fan experiences. For shows with a significant following, this can be a substantial source of revenue.

The use of reality TV as a marketing platform for other products and services is another economic aspect. For example, music competition shows can launch the careers of new artists, who then generate revenue through album sales, concerts, and merchandise. Similarly, cooking shows can boost the sales of cookbooks and kitchen products.

However, the economics of reality TV are not without challenges. Audience tastes can be fickle, and shows that fail to capture or maintain viewer interest can quickly become financial burdens. The competitive landscape of television and streaming platforms also means that reality TV shows must constantly innovate to remain relevant and profitable.

In conclusion, the economics of reality TV are characterized by low production costs, diverse revenue streams, and high audience engagement. This combination makes it a financially attractive genre for networks and producers. However, the need to adapt to changing viewer preferences and the competitive media environment requires strategic planning and continuous innovation to sustain economic success. Reality TV, in its essence, is not just a cultural phenomenon but also a significant economic player in the entertainment industry.

Chapter 27: Reality TV around the World

The global appeal of reality TV has led to its widespread proliferation and adaptation across various cultures and countries. This chapter explores the international landscape of reality TV, examining how different regions have embraced and adapted the genre to reflect local cultures, tastes, and societal norms.

Reality TV's global journey is marked by the adaptation of popular formats to suit local audiences. Formats like 'Big Brother', 'Survivor', and 'The Voice' have seen numerous international versions, each tailored to the cultural context of the country. These adaptations often involve tweaking the show's rules, presentation, and participant selection to resonate with local viewers. For instance, while the core concept of 'Big Brother' remains constant, the challenges, themes, and interactions are often reflective of the host country's societal values and humor.

In addition to adaptations, many countries have developed their own unique reality TV formats. These original shows often highlight specific aspects of the country's culture, such as traditional arts, regional cuisines, or unique lifestyles. For example, in Japan, reality shows often focus on minimalism, discipline, and endurance, while in India, they may center around Bollywood dance competitions or family-centric dramas.

The impact of cultural differences on reality TV is significant. In some regions, conservative cultural norms influence the content and presentation of reality shows, with modesty and respect being key considerations. In contrast, Western reality shows often push the boundaries of what is considered acceptable on television, with a focus on sensationalism and individualism.

The popularity of reality TV has also led to a blending of cultures. International audiences are exposed to different ways of life, traditions, and social norms, fostering a greater understanding and appreciation of diversity. This cross-cultural exchange can be a powerful tool for breaking down stereotypes and promoting global connectedness.

However, the globalization of reality TV also raises concerns about cultural homogenization. The dominance of certain formats and the influence of Western media can overshadow local entertainment traditions, potentially leading to a loss of cultural diversity in television programming.

In conclusion, reality TV around the world reflects the diversity and complexity of global cultures. While the genre has the power to unify audiences across borders, it also highlights the unique characteristics of different societies. The internationalization of reality TV is a testament to its adaptability and appeal, offering a window into the varied and vibrant tapestry of global cultures. As reality TV continues to evolve, it will likely keep playing a significant role in shaping and reflecting cultural narratives across the world.

Chapter 28: From Idea to Airwaves: The Production Timeline

The journey of a reality TV show from its initial conception to broadcast is a complex and multifaceted process. This chapter outlines the typical production timeline for a reality TV show, providing insight into the various stages involved in turning a creative idea into a televised reality.

Idea Development and Conceptualization: The inception of a reality TV show begins with an idea. This idea is then fleshed out into a viable concept, involving decisions about the show's format, target audience, and unique selling points. This stage often includes market research to gauge potential viewer interest and to identify any similar existing shows.

Pitching and Greenlighting: Once the concept is developed, it is pitched to television networks or production companies. This involves presenting the concept, explaining its appeal, and demonstrating its potential success. If the pitch is successful, the show is greenlit, and funding is secured, either from the network, sponsors, or through other financing means.

Pre-production: This phase involves detailed planning and preparation. Key activities include casting, scouting and securing locations, hiring crew, and finalizing the show's format and rules. For international or travel-based shows, this stage also involves logistical arrangements like travel planning and obtaining necessary permits and clearances.

Casting: Casting is a critical component of the production timeline. It typically involves a public call for participants, screening applications, conducting auditions and interviews, and finally selecting the cast. This process can be time-consuming, as it requires finding the right mix of personalities to create an engaging and dynamic show.

Filming: The filming stage is when the actual production takes place. Depending on the format, this can range from a few days to several months. During this time, the crew captures footage according to the episode outlines, often working long hours and in challenging conditions. Reality TV filming usually requires a flexible approach to accommodate unscripted events and spontaneous participant actions.

Post-production: Post-production is where the show really comes together. This stage involves reviewing and editing the footage to create episodes, adding music and special effects, and finalizing the narrative. Editors play a crucial role in shaping how the show will be perceived by the audience.

Marketing and Promotion: Concurrently with post-production, the marketing and promotion phase kicks in. This includes creating trailers, engaging in social media promotion, and possibly hosting press events or sneak peeks. The aim is to generate buzz and anticipation for the show.

Broadcasting: Finally, the show airs on television. This might involve a weekly broadcast schedule or, in the case of some streaming services, releasing an entire season at once. The success of the show during this phase is closely monitored through ratings and viewer feedback.

Post-Air Analysis and Follow-Up: After the show has aired, producers and networks often analyze its performance. This includes reviewing ratings, social media engagement, and critical feedback. This analysis can inform decisions about potential future seasons or spin-offs.

In conclusion, the production timeline of a reality TV show is a lengthy and intricate process involving a myriad of steps from the initial idea to the final broadcast. Each stage requires careful planning, coordination, and a talented team of professionals dedicated to creating engaging and successful television content.

Chapter 29: Controversies and Scandals in Reality TV

Reality TV, with its blend of real-life drama and entertainment, is no stranger to controversies and scandals. This chapter examines the various types of controversies that have arisen in the genre, exploring their causes, consequences, and the broader implications they hold for reality TV as a form of media.

One common source of controversy in reality TV is the portrayal of participants. Issues arise when participants are depicted in a way that is misleading, overly negative, or exploitative. Such portrayals can lead to public backlash, damage to participants' reputations, and even legal repercussions. Shows have faced criticism for selectively editing footage to create 'villains' or 'heroes', sparking debates about ethical editing and the responsibilities of producers.

Another area of controversy is the staging or scripting of events. While reality TV is supposed to depict real-life events, some shows have been accused of scripting scenarios or encouraging participants to act in certain ways to create drama. This raises questions about the authenticity of the genre and can lead to viewer disillusionment.

The psychological and physical well-being of participants is a significant concern. There have been instances where the intense environment of reality TV has led to mental health issues or stress-induced conditions among participants. The ethical considerations of placing individuals in high-pressure, highly scrutinized environments are a topic of ongoing debate.

Reality TV shows have also been embroiled in legal controversies. These range from breaches of contract and labor laws to more serious allegations like assault or harassment. Such incidents not only affect the individuals involved but can also tarnish the reputation of the show and the network. The handling of sensitive topics is another area prone to controversy. Shows that deal with issues like race, sexuality, or addiction can sometimes be seen as trivializing or mishandling these topics. This can lead to public outcry and demands for more responsible and respectful treatment of serious issues.

The impact of reality TV on societal norms and behaviors is a broader area of controversy. Critics argue that some shows promote unhealthy values, such as materialism, aggression, or unrealistic body standards. This has sparked discussions about the social responsibility of reality TV producers and networks.

In conclusion, controversies and scandals are almost inherent to the nature of reality TV, given its focus on real people and unscripted events. These controversies often reflect larger societal issues and can have significant implications for the participants, producers, and viewers. They highlight the need for ethical production practices, responsible handling of sensitive topics, and consideration for the well-being of participants. As reality TV continues to evolve, navigating these controversies will be crucial in maintaining the integrity and sustainability of the genre.

Chapter 30: The Future of Reality TV
As we look towards the future, reality TV stands at a crossroads, shaped by evolving technologies, changing viewer preferences, and broader societal trends. This chapter explores potential developments and innovations in the genre, offering insights into what the future might hold for reality TV.

Technological Advancements: Emerging technologies like virtual reality (VR) and augmented reality (AR) could revolutionize how audiences experience reality TV. Imagine donning a VR headset to immerse yourself in the environment of a survival show or using AR to interact with elements of a cooking competition in real-time. Such technologies could create more interactive and engaging viewer experiences.

Increased Viewer Interaction: The trend towards viewer participation is likely to intensify. With the rise of digital platforms, we may see more shows incorporating real-time voting, audience-driven storylines, and interactive challenges. This shift could transform viewers from passive consumers into active participants in the reality TV narrative.

Diverse Content and Representation: As audiences become more global and diverse, there will be a growing demand for inclusive content that reflects a wider range of experiences and backgrounds. This could lead to more shows focusing on underrepresented communities, exploring global cultures, and tackling a broader array of social issues.

Ethical and Responsible Production: With increasing awareness of the psychological impact of reality TV on participants, there will likely be a push for more ethical production practices. This could involve better support systems for participants, more transparent editing practices, and a focus on the respectful treatment of sensitive issues.

Blending Genres: The future of reality TV may see a blending of genres, merging documentary-style storytelling with traditional reality formats. This hybrid approach could offer deeper insights into real-world issues while maintaining the entertainment value that draws viewers to reality TV.

Sustainability and Environmental Awareness: As global concerns about sustainability grow, reality TV might adapt to reflect these issues. We could see shows focusing on eco-friendly living, conservation efforts, or sustainable travel, aligning the genre with broader environmental and social movements.

Localized and Hyper-Niche Content: The success of streaming platforms and on-demand viewing could lead to more localized and niche reality shows. Catering to specific interests and communities, these shows might not have mass appeal but could be intensely popular within certain segments of the audience.

In conclusion, the future of reality TV is likely to be characterized by technological innovation, increased interactivity, diverse content, and ethical production practices. As the genre continues to adapt to changing times and technologies, it holds the potential to remain a significant and influential part of the entertainment landscape, offering new ways for audiences to engage with the blurred lines between reality and television.

Chapter 31: Cross-Platform Storytelling in Reality Shows

Cross-platform storytelling represents a dynamic shift in the landscape of reality TV, where the narrative extends beyond the traditional confines of television broadcasting. This chapter explores how reality shows are leveraging multiple platforms to enrich storytelling, enhance viewer engagement, and create a more immersive experience.

Integration with Digital Media: The integration of social media platforms like Twitter, Instagram, and Facebook has become integral to the storytelling of reality shows. These platforms allow for real-time updates, behind-the-scenes content, and additional storylines that complement the main show. They also enable viewers to interact directly with show participants and producers, creating a two-way dialogue that enriches the viewing experience.

Web Series and Spin-offs: Many reality shows extend their narrative through web series, blogs, or podcasts that delve deeper into specific aspects of the show or explore the lives of participants after the main show has ended. These spin-offs provide additional content for die-hard fans and keep the audience engaged beyond the show's television airing.

Interactive Apps and Online Games: The use of interactive apps and online games allows viewers to engage with the reality show in a more hands-on manner. For example, viewers might participate in virtual challenges related to the show, vote on outcomes, or even influence the direction of the show through interactive decision-making features.

User-Generated Content: Encouraging user-generated content is another facet of cross-platform storytelling. Reality shows often prompt viewers to share their own stories, videos, or reactions related to the show's theme. This not only increases viewer engagement but also adds a layer of community storytelling to the show's narrative.

Virtual and Augmented Reality Experiences: As technology advances, reality shows are beginning to experiment with virtual and augmented reality. These technologies offer viewers an immersive experience, such as exploring the show's set in virtual reality or augmenting their viewing environment with relevant digital content.

Real-Time Interaction and Live Streaming: Live streaming and real-time interaction features provide audiences with a sense of immediacy and involvement. Shows might feature live Q&A sessions, streaming of unedited footage, or live reactions to events, creating a more dynamic and immediate connection between the show and its audience.

E-commerce Integration: Some reality shows integrate e-commerce platforms, allowing viewers to purchase products featured in the show. This not only serves as a revenue stream but also adds a tangible aspect to the viewing experience, as viewers can own a piece of the show.
In conclusion, cross-platform storytelling in reality shows is transforming how audiences consume and interact with television content. By extending the narrative across multiple digital platforms, reality TV can offer a more engaging, interactive, and immersive experience. This multi-dimensional approach not only keeps viewers invested in the show's universe but also paves the way for innovative storytelling techniques in the realm of reality TV.

Chapter 32: The Psychological Impact on Contestants

Participating in a reality TV show can be a life-changing experience, often accompanied by significant psychological impacts on contestants. This chapter delves into the various psychological effects that participants may experience during and after their time on a reality show, exploring the challenges they face and the support mechanisms that can be beneficial.

Adjustment to the Reality TV Environment: Contestants often undergo a drastic shift from their normal lives to a highly controlled and scrutinized environment. The constant presence of cameras, the pressure of competitions, and living with strangers can be stressful and disorienting. This adjustment period can be mentally challenging, as contestants grapple with loss of privacy and heightened stress.

Impact of Public Scrutiny and Fame: Participants in reality TV shows can become public figures overnight, subject to intense scrutiny and judgment from viewers and media. This sudden fame can lead to psychological pressures, including anxiety, self-esteem issues, and a distorted sense of self-worth. The often-temporary nature of this fame can also result in difficulties adjusting back to normal life post-show.

Social Dynamics and Isolation: The intense social dynamics within reality TV shows can also have psychological impacts. Contestants may experience isolation, bullying, or pressure to conform to group norms. The competitive nature of many shows can lead to strained relationships and trust issues, both during and after the show.

Post-Show Adjustment and Reintegration: After the show, contestants may struggle to reintegrate into their regular lives. They may face challenges in resuming their previous routines, relationships, and careers, especially if they have been portrayed negatively or have experienced significant public attention.

Positive Psychological Impacts: While there are challenges, participation in reality TV can also have positive effects. Contestants may experience personal growth, increased self-awareness, and development of new skills or talents. The show can be a platform for advancing their careers or advocating for causes they are passionate about.

Support and Aftercare: Given these potential psychological impacts, providing support and aftercare for contestants is crucial. This can include psychological counseling, media training, and support in managing public attention post-show. Some shows have implemented regular check-ins with psychologists during and after filming to support contestants' mental health.

Ethical Considerations in Casting and Production: Ethical considerations are vital in the casting and production process. This includes ensuring that contestants are mentally prepared for the experience, transparent about the nature of the show, and not exploited for sensational content. Producers have a responsibility to create a safe and respectful environment for participants.

In conclusion, the psychological impact on contestants of reality TV shows is multifaceted, encompassing both challenges and opportunities for personal growth. Understanding and addressing these psychological effects is essential for the well-being of participants. Providing adequate support and aftercare, along with ethical production practices, can help mitigate negative impacts and enhance the positive aspects of participating in reality TV.

Chapter 33: Celebrity and Fame: The Aftermath of Reality TV

The aftermath of participating in a reality TV show often catapults contestants into the limelight, navigating the complex world of newfound fame and celebrity status. This chapter examines the trajectory of reality TV participants post-show, exploring the impact of sudden fame, the opportunities and challenges it brings, and how it shapes their future paths.

Instant Celebrity Status: Participants on popular reality TV shows can gain instant celebrity status, attracting significant media attention and a large following on social media. This sudden shift from anonymity to fame can be overwhelming, requiring participants to quickly adapt to being in the public eye and manage their public image.

Opportunities and Career Prospects: Reality TV fame can open doors to various opportunities, from media appearances and endorsements to roles in other TV shows or entertainment projects. Some participants leverage their fame to launch careers in acting, music, or as influencers. For others, the platform can be used to promote personal businesses, causes, or pursue professional goals aligned with their newfound public profile.

Challenges and Pressures: The flip side of reality TV fame includes facing public scrutiny, criticism, and invasion of privacy. Participants may find their every action analyzed and judged, leading to stress and impact on their mental health. Adjusting to the ebb and flow of fame, especially as the initial buzz fades, can be challenging for many.

Financial Implications: The financial impact of reality TV fame varies. While some contestants may capitalize on their fame for financial gain through endorsements and public appearances, others may struggle to monetize their newfound celebrity status. Managing finances, especially with the uncertainty of how long the fame will last, can be a complex aspect for many participants.

Navigating Relationships: Relationships, both personal and professional, can be affected by the fame that comes with reality TV. Participants may find that their relationships with family and friends change, and they may face difficulties in forming new relationships due to their public persona.

Typecasting and Long-Term Prospects: Reality TV participants often face the risk of being typecast, which can limit their future career opportunities in the entertainment industry. Finding roles or opportunities that diverge from their reality TV persona can be a significant challenge for those looking to build a long-term career in entertainment.

Life after the Limelight: As the immediate fame subsides, participants face the task of figuring out their next steps. This may involve returning to their previous careers or lifestyles, or reinventing themselves to maintain public interest. The transition from being in the limelight to a more regular life can be a period of significant adjustment.

In conclusion, the aftermath of reality TV fame encompasses a spectrum of experiences, from exciting opportunities to challenging adjustments. The trajectory of participants post-show is influenced by various factors, including how they manage their public image, the support systems they have, and their personal resilience. Navigating the complex landscape of celebrity and fame is a critical aspect of the reality TV experience, often shaping the future paths of those who participate in these shows.

Chapter 34: Reality TV: A Cultural Analysis

Reality TV, as a cultural phenomenon, offers a rich field for analysis, reflecting and shaping societal values, norms, and behaviors. This chapter provides a cultural analysis of reality TV, exploring how the genre mirrors societal trends, influences public discourse, and serves as a barometer for changing cultural dynamics.

Reflection of Societal Trends: Reality TV often acts as a mirror to society, showcasing trends, issues, and values prevalent in contemporary culture. Shows focusing on social experiments, lifestyle changes, or competition formats reveal much about societal norms and ideals, such as success, beauty, and relationships. This reflection can either reinforce or challenge existing cultural norms.

Influence on Public Discourse: Reality TV has a significant impact on public discourse, often sparking conversations about important social issues. Topics like mental health, body image, race, and gender dynamics are frequently brought to the forefront through these shows, facilitating wider societal discussions and sometimes even leading to changes in public attitudes.

Role in Shaping Cultural Norms: The genre plays an active role in shaping cultural norms and behaviors. Reality TV can normalize certain lifestyles or behaviors and make them more acceptable in mainstream culture. For instance, shows that celebrate diverse identities and lifestyles can foster greater acceptance and understanding of different communities.

Globalization and Cultural Exchange: The international nature of reality TV contributes to cultural exchange and globalization. As formats are adapted in different countries, they often incorporate local cultural elements, providing viewers with insights into other cultures and ways of life. This exchange can promote a more interconnected and global cultural landscape.

Commercialization and Consumer Culture: Reality TV is also intertwined with commercialization and consumer culture. Product placements, branding, and celebrity endorsements within shows reflect and amplify consumerist values, making the genre a powerful tool for marketing and advertising.

Representation and Stereotyping: The way individuals and groups are represented in reality TV is a key area of cultural analysis. While the genre can offer visibility to diverse groups, it can also perpetuate stereotypes and simplistic narratives. The representation in these shows thus has broader implications for how groups are viewed in society.

Ethical and Moral Considerations: Reality TV raises various ethical and moral considerations, such as the exploitation of participants, the blurring of entertainment and reality, and the impact of these shows on participants and viewers. These considerations reflect broader societal debates about media ethics and the role of entertainment in public life.

In conclusion, a cultural analysis of reality TV reveals its multifaceted impact on society. The genre not only reflects cultural norms and values but also actively shapes them. It plays a significant role in influencing public discourse, promoting cultural exchange, and reflecting broader societal trends. As reality TV continues to evolve, its role as a cultural barometer and influencer is likely to remain a subject of interest and analysis.

Chapter 35: The Legacy of Iconic Reality TV Shows

Iconic reality TV shows have left indelible marks on the cultural landscape, influencing television programming, societal norms, and even the way we view our own realities. This chapter explores the legacy of some of the most influential reality TV shows, examining their impact on entertainment, society, and the enduring fascination they hold.

Pioneering Formats: Shows like 'Survivor', 'Big Brother', and 'The Real World' pioneered formats that became blueprints for countless reality TV shows that followed. They introduced the concepts of social experiment, continuous surveillance, and competitive elimination, which have become staples in the genre. Their innovative formats expanded the boundaries of television storytelling, creating new possibilities for audience engagement and narrative development.

Cultural Phenomena: Certain reality shows transcended the realm of entertainment to become cultural phenomena. 'American Idol', for example, not only dominated television ratings but also significantly impacted the music industry, launching the careers of numerous artists. Similarly, shows like 'Keeping Up with the Kardashians' have influenced fashion, social media trends, and the concept of celebrity in the 21st century.

Social Commentary and Change: Some iconic reality shows have contributed to social commentary and change. They have brought important issues to the forefront, from race and class to sexuality and body image, often sparking national conversations and challenging societal norms. For instance,

'Queer Eye' has been praised for its positive representation of the LGBTQ+ community and its role in promoting acceptance and understanding.

Global Reach and Adaptation: The international adaptation of iconic reality shows demonstrates their universal appeal and cultural impact. Formats like 'MasterChef' and 'Got Talent' have been localized in numerous countries, each version reflecting the unique cultural nuances of its region. This global reach has not only entertained but also fostered a sense of global community and cultural exchange.

Influence on Viewer Behavior and Interaction: Iconic reality shows have changed the way viewers interact with television. The integration of audience voting, social media engagement, and online fan communities has made viewing a more interactive and participatory experience. These shows have paved the way for a more engaged and vocal audience, influencing how media content is consumed and discussed.

Reflection of Societal Values: The enduring popularity of certain reality shows offers insights into the values and interests of society at different times. They reflect and sometimes challenge prevailing attitudes, offering a window into the evolving dynamics of societal values and norms.

Challenges and Criticisms: The legacy of these shows also includes the controversies and criticisms they have faced, from accusations of scripted content to concerns about participant welfare and the ethics of reality TV. These challenges have sparked important conversations about media responsibility and consumer awareness.

In conclusion, the legacy of iconic reality TV shows is multifaceted, spanning entertainment, culture, and social discourse. These shows have not only provided entertainment but also influenced societal trends, media consumption patterns, and the global television landscape. As reality TV continues to evolve, the legacy of these iconic shows serves as a testament to the genre's significant impact on both entertainment and society.

An Analysis of 10 Successful Reality TV Shows

These shows have made significant contributions to the reality TV genre, each in its own way. They have entertained audiences, sparked conversations, and left a lasting legacy on television and popular culture.

Queer Eye

"Queer Eye" is an American reality television series that was initially released on February 7, 2018, on Netflix. It is a reboot of the original 2003 series produced by Bravo. The show is known for its unique concept, where each episode features five advisors known as the "Fab Five" who spend a week applying their expertise to help improve someone's life situation. The Fab Five consists of experts in various fields:

1. Antoni Porowski - Food and Wine: He specializes in alcohol and food preparation.
2. Bobby Berk - Design: He is an expert in interior design and home organization.
3. Jonathan Van Ness - Grooming: His expertise lies in hair, personal hygiene, and makeup.
4. Karamo Brown - Culture and Lifestyle: Karamo is an expert on relationships and social interaction.
5. Tan France - Fashion: He specializes in clothing, fashion, and personal styling.

The show has received acclaim for its strong representation of the LGBTQ+ community and its positive impact on the lives of the individuals featured in each episode. It has successfully broadcasted 65 episodes with the seventh season released in May 2023.

Additionally, "Queer Eye" has inspired adaptations in other countries, including a German adaptation and a Brazilian adaptation. The series has continued to evolve, with plans for a ninth season set to be filmed in Las Vegas.

The show's format involves transforming various aspects of the participants' lives, from their personal style and grooming to their living spaces and overall well-being. Each episode focuses on one individual, referred to as the "hero," and the Fab Five work together to bring about positive changes in their lives.

"Queer Eye" has not only entertained viewers but has also highlighted the importance of self-care, self-expression, and self-improvement. It has resonated with audiences for its heartwarming stories and the genuine care shown by the Fab Five towards the heroes they assist.

Survivor

Number of Episodes or Years of Production: "Survivor" had been in production for over 20 years. It originally premiered in 2000 and continued to produce multiple seasons annually. Each season typically consists of around 13 to 16 episodes.

Costs of Production: The costs of production for "Survivor" can vary from season to season. Expenses include location scouting, crew salaries, contestant stipends, equipment, and more. The show is known for its exotic filming locations, which can contribute significantly to production costs.

Number of Viewers: "Survivor" has been a consistently popular show with a substantial viewership. In its early seasons, it attracted millions of viewers per episode. The number of viewers may have fluctuated over the years, but it has maintained a dedicated fan base.

Costs to Set Up and Run: Setting up "Survivor" involves selecting and preparing a remote location, assembling a production crew, casting contestants, and acquiring the necessary equipment. The costs to set up and run the show can be substantial, but it is offset by advertising revenue and sponsorships.

Ratings: "Survivor" has generally received positive ratings from both critics and viewers. Its unique format, which combines elements of competition, strategy, and social dynamics, has been praised for its entertainment value and suspenseful storytelling. The show has won numerous awards and nominations over the years.

Detailed Description of the Show: "Survivor" is a reality television competition show where a group of contestants, usually around 16 to 20 individuals, are marooned in a remote location, often an island or wilderness area. They must work together to provide food, shelter, and necessities while competing in various challenges.

The core premise of "Survivor" revolves around the contestants forming alliances, strategizing, and ultimately voting each other out at tribal council meetings. The last remaining contestant, known as the "Sole Survivor," wins a substantial cash prize.

The show is known for its physical challenges, mental strategy, and the social dynamics that develop among the contestants. It often explores themes of trust, deception, and the lengths people will go to in order to win.

Jeff Probst has been the long-time host and face of "Survivor," guiding the contestants and providing commentary throughout the seasons.

Please note that for the most current information, including the number of episodes and recent developments in "Survivor," I recommend checking the latest sources or the official "Survivor" website.

Big Brother

Number of Episodes or Years of Production: "Big Brother" is a long-running reality TV show that has been produced in numerous countries worldwide. It originally premiered in the Netherlands in 1999 and has since been adapted in over 60 countries. Each season typically consists of multiple episodes, with the duration varying depending on the country's format. Some seasons can last for several months.

Costs of Production: The costs of production for "Big Brother" can vary significantly depending on the country and the scale of the production. Expenses include location costs, crew salaries, contestant stipends, technology for 24/7 live feeds, and the construction and maintenance of the Big Brother house. The show is known for its unique house design and advanced surveillance technology.

Number of Viewers: "Big Brother" has had a substantial viewership in many countries, with millions of viewers tuning in to watch the show. The number of viewers can vary from season to season and country to country but has maintained a dedicated fan base over the years.

Costs to Set Up and Run: Setting up and running "Big Brother" involves selecting a suitable location, constructing the Big Brother house, recruiting contestants, hiring production staff, and ensuring 24/7 live feeds and surveillance equipment are in place. The costs can be substantial, but they are typically covered by advertising revenue, sponsorships, and international licensing deals.

Ratings: "Big Brother" has received mixed reviews from critics over the years. It is known for its unique format, which combines elements of competition, strategy, and social dynamics. The show has been praised for its ability to create suspense and drama as contestants are isolated and constantly monitored. However, it has also faced criticism for controversies related to contestant behavior and privacy concerns.

Detailed Description of the Show: "Big Brother" is a reality TV competition show where a group of contestants, known as housemates, live together in a specially designed house equipped with cameras and microphones. The housemates are isolated from the outside world and are constantly under surveillance.

The core premise of "Big Brother" involves the housemates participating in various challenges and tasks while forming alliances and strategic partnerships. Housemates are evicted from the house through a voting process conducted by their fellow housemates, with the last remaining housemate winning a cash prize.

The show is known for its 24/7 live feeds, which allow viewers to watch the housemates' interactions in real-time. This aspect of constant surveillance adds an extra layer of intrigue and engagement for fans.

"Big Brother" is hosted by a presenter who interacts with the housemates and announces evictions and challenges. The show often explores themes of trust, strategy, and the psychological impact of isolation.

Please note that the specifics of "Big Brother" can vary from country to country due to the different adaptations and formats. For the most up-to-date information on the show's production details and ratings, I recommend checking the latest sources or the official "Big Brother" website for your region.

The Real World

Number of Episodes or Years of Production: "The Real World" is a pioneering reality TV show that originally premiered in 1992. It was produced by MTV and has a long history of seasons, with each season typically consisting of multiple episodes. The show's format often involves casting a group of young adults who live together in a house for a specific period while their experiences are filmed.

Costs of Production: The costs of production for "The Real World" can vary depending on the location of the house, crew salaries, and other logistical expenses. While it may not have the same level of production costs as some other reality shows with elaborate sets and challenges, it still requires a significant budget for filming and editing.

Number of Viewers: "The Real World" has had a dedicated viewership over the years. It became a cultural phenomenon during its early seasons and attracted a substantial audience. The number of viewers may have fluctuated over time, but it has remained influential in the reality TV genre.

Costs to Set Up and Run: Setting up and running "The Real World" involves selecting a suitable city and house location, casting diverse housemates, hiring a production crew, and covering the costs of filming and editing. While it may not have the same level of competition and challenges as other reality shows, it still requires funding for its unique format.

Legacy: "The Real World" holds a significant legacy in the reality TV genre. It is considered one of the first reality shows of its kind, setting the template for many future reality TV programs. The show's format of bringing together a diverse group of individuals with varying backgrounds and personalities living together in close quarters has influenced numerous other reality shows.

Additionally, "The Real World" was known for addressing social issues and tackling real-life problems faced by its housemates. It often featured discussions on topics such as race, gender, sexuality, and cultural differences, making it a pioneer in using reality TV as a platform for social commentary.

The show's legacy includes the impact it had on the way reality TV portrays real-life situations and the way it engages with important societal issues. It paved the way for more socially conscious reality programming.

Detailed Description of the Show: "The Real World" is a reality TV series that follows the lives of a group of young adults, typically aged 18 to 29, who come from diverse backgrounds and live together in a shared house. The housemates are selected based on their different personalities, backgrounds, and life experiences, which often lead to conflicts and drama.

The show is known for its unscripted format, allowing the housemates to interact naturally while their experiences are filmed. Each season focuses on the interactions, relationships, and personal growth of the housemates as they navigate their daily lives and confront various challenges.

"The Real World" is known for its "confessional" style interviews, where housemates share their thoughts and feelings directly with the camera. This format allows viewers to gain insight into the housemates' perspectives and emotions.

Over the years, "The Real World" has been set in various cities across the United States and occasionally in international locations.

Please note that "The Real World" has gone through various changes and adaptations over the years, and the specifics of each season may vary. For the most up-to-date information on the show's production details and its impact on reality TV, you may refer to sources from MTV or other reliable sources.

American Idol

Number of Episodes or Years of Production: "American Idol" is a highly successful singing competition reality TV show that first premiered in the United States in 2002. It has had numerous seasons, with each season consisting of multiple episodes. Over the years, it became an annual event that showcased aspiring singers.

Costs of Production: The costs of production for "American Idol" can be substantial. Expenses include securing a venue for auditions and live shows, recruiting a panel of celebrity judges, production crew salaries, contestant stipends, and elaborate stage and set designs. The show's high production values contribute to its entertainment quality.

Number of Viewers: "American Idol" has consistently attracted a large and dedicated viewership. In its early seasons, it was a cultural phenomenon in the United States, regularly drawing tens of millions of viewers per episode. While viewership may have fluctuated over the years, it remains a prominent show in the reality competition genre.

Costs to Set Up and Run: Setting up and running "American Idol" involves a comprehensive process. Auditions are held in multiple cities across the country, requiring logistics, venue rentals, and security. The show also covers travel and accommodation expenses for contestants who make it to Hollywood Week. The live shows involve advanced stage and lighting setups. However, the costs are offset by advertising revenue and sponsorships.

Legacy: "American Idol" has left an enduring legacy in the entertainment industry. It is credited with launching the careers of major artists, including Kelly Clarkson, Carrie Underwood, and Jennifer Hudson, among others. The show's format of a singing competition with viewer voting has become a blueprint for numerous music competition shows worldwide.

Additionally, "American Idol" played a significant role in reshaping the music industry by providing a platform for emerging artists to gain recognition and record deals. It also popularized the concept of audience participation through voting, which became a common feature in modern music competition shows.

Detailed Description of the Show: "American Idol" is a singing competition reality TV show where aspiring singers from various backgrounds and vocal genres compete for the title of the "American Idol." The show typically follows a structured format:

Auditions: Contestants audition in front of a panel of celebrity judges in different cities across the United States. These auditions are known for showcasing a wide range of talent, from exceptional singers to comically bad performances.

Hollywood Week: Contestants who receive a "golden ticket" advance to Hollywood Week, where they face more challenges and intense competition.

Live Shows: The remaining contestants perform live on television, and viewers vote for their favorite contestants. Contestants are gradually eliminated until the final rounds.

Grand Finale: The show culminates in a grand finale where the winner is crowned the "American Idol." The winner typically receives a recording contract and various opportunities in the music industry.

"American Idol" is known for its celebrity judges, who provide feedback and critiques to contestants. The show has featured a rotating panel of judges over the years, including notable names from the music industry.

Beyond being a singing competition, "American Idol" also showcases the personal journeys and stories of contestants, adding an emotional element to the show.

For the most up-to-date information on the show's production details and its impact on the music industry, you may refer to official sources or credible entertainment news outlets.

Keeping Up with the Kardashians

Number of Episodes or Years of Production: "Keeping Up with the Kardashians" is a reality television series that premiered in 2007 and concluded in 2021. It ran for 20 seasons, with each season consisting of multiple episodes. The show had a long and successful run, documenting the lives of the Kardashian-Jenner family over the years.

Costs of Production: The costs of production for "Keeping Up with the Kardashians" included the salaries of the Kardashian-Jenner family members, production crew expenses, filming locations, and the costs associated with creating and editing each episode. As the show became more popular, the family's compensation increased substantially.

Number of Viewers: "Keeping Up with the Kardashians" was a highly popular reality TV show with a dedicated fan base. It consistently attracted millions of viewers per episode during its run. The show's viewership contributed to the family's rise to fame.

Costs to Set Up and Run: While the show did not require elaborate set designs or competition formats, it did incur costs associated with filming in various locations, maintaining a production team, and promoting the show. The family's lifestyle and experiences also contributed to the costs of the show.

Legacy: "Keeping Up with the Kardashians" had a profound impact on celebrity culture and the entertainment industry. Its legacy includes redefining the concept of celebrity in the 21st century. The show's success demonstrated that individuals could become global celebrities through reality TV and strategic use of social media.

Additionally, the Kardashian-Jenner family's influence on fashion, beauty, and pop culture cannot be understated. They launched successful businesses, fashion lines, and beauty brands, making them influential figures in the beauty and fashion industries.

The show's emphasis on family dynamics, personal relationships, and the vulnerabilities of its cast members also contributed to its impact. It allowed viewers to connect with the family on a personal level, humanizing celebrities in a way that was not typical in the entertainment industry.

Detailed Description of the Show: "Keeping Up with the Kardashians" is a docuseries that follows the lives of the Kardashian-Jenner family, which includes Kris Jenner, her children Kourtney, Kim, Khloé, and Rob Kardashian, and her daughters Kendall and Kylie Jenner. The show provides an inside look into their personal lives, relationships, and careers.

The format of the show involves capturing various aspects of the family's lives, including their daily interactions, business endeavors, fashion ventures, and personal challenges. It also chronicles major life events, such as weddings, births, and divorces.

"Keeping Up with the Kardashians" is known for its candid moments, emotional discussions, and the family's willingness to share both their successes and struggles with the audience. The show's authenticity and relatability played a significant role in its popularity.

Beyond the television series, the Kardashian-Jenner family leveraged their fame to launch successful businesses, including fashion lines, beauty products, and mobile apps. They became influential figures in the world of entertainment, fashion, and beauty.

Please note that while "Keeping Up with the Kardashians" concluded its original series in 2021, individual family members have continued to engage in various ventures and projects, maintaining their presence in the media and entertainment industry.

MasterChef

Number of Episodes or Years of Production: "MasterChef" is a culinary competition reality TV show that originated in the United Kingdom and has been adapted in numerous countries around the world. It has had multiple seasons in each country, with each season typically consisting of several episodes. The show's success has led to the creation of various international versions.

Costs of Production: The costs of production for "MasterChef" can vary depending on the scale and production values of each adaptation. Expenses include securing a location for challenges and eliminations, contestant accommodations, sourcing ingredients, salaries for judges and crew, and the set design for the kitchen. The show's focus on food quality and presentation contributes to its production costs.

Number of Viewers: "MasterChef" has attracted a significant viewership in multiple countries. It appeals to a wide audience, from food enthusiasts to those interested in culinary competitions. The number of viewers can vary by country and season but has consistently maintained a dedicated fan base.

Costs to Set Up and Run: Setting up and running "MasterChef" involves a comprehensive process. Contestants are selected through auditions, and the show often includes various cooking challenges, mystery box challenges, and elimination rounds. The costs also include the prize awarded to the winner, which can be a cash prize or other culinary opportunities.

Legacy: "MasterChef" has left a lasting legacy in the world of culinary television. It has inspired countless individuals to pursue their passion for cooking and has popularized the genre of culinary competitions. The show's format, which features amateur chefs competing in a high-stakes culinary environment, has become a blueprint for many other cooking shows.

Additionally, "MasterChef" has played a role in promoting the appreciation of food, culinary skills, and creativity in the kitchen. It has elevated cooking to an art form and showcased the potential of home cooks to achieve culinary excellence.

Detailed Description of the Show: "MasterChef" is a culinary competition reality TV series that features amateur chefs from various backgrounds and skill levels. The show typically follows a structured format:

Auditions: Contestants audition for a coveted spot on the show by presenting a signature dish to a panel of judges. Those who impress the judges move on to the competition.

Challenges: The competition consists of various culinary challenges, including mystery box challenges, team challenges, and elimination rounds. Contestants are tasked with creating dishes under time constraints and using specific ingredients.

Judging: A panel of culinary experts, often including celebrity chefs, evaluates the dishes based on taste, presentation, and creativity. Contestants receive feedback and scores from the judges.

Eliminations: After each challenge, one or more contestants may be eliminated from the competition. The goal is to narrow down the field until a winner is determined.

Finale: The show culminates in a grand finale where the finalists compete for the title of "MasterChef" and the associated prize.

"MasterChef" is known for its emphasis on culinary skill, creativity, and the journey of amateur chefs as they strive to improve their cooking abilities. It also showcases the diversity of cuisines and cooking techniques from around the world.

Please note that "MasterChef" may have continued to produce new seasons or special editions since my last research, so for the most up-to-date information on the show, you may refer to official sources or streaming platforms where the show is available.

The Bachelor and "The Bachelorette

Number of Episodes or Years of Production: "The Bachelor" and "The Bachelorette" are dating competition reality TV shows with long and ongoing histories. "The Bachelor" first premiered in 2002, while "The Bachelorette" premiered in 2003. Both shows have had numerous seasons, with each season consisting of multiple episodes. The franchise has expanded over the years to include spin-offs like "Bachelor in Paradise" and "Bachelor Pad."

Costs of Production: The costs of production for "The Bachelor" and "The Bachelorette" can be substantial. Expenses include securing luxurious filming locations, travel expenses for the cast and crew, salaries for the bachelor or bachelorette, contestant accommodations, and production crew salaries. The elaborate dates and activities featured in the show also contribute to its production costs.

Number of Viewers: Both "The Bachelor" and "The Bachelorette" have consistently attracted a large viewership over the years. The shows appeal to audiences interested in romance, drama, and dating competitions. While viewership numbers can vary by season, the shows maintain dedicated fan bases.

Costs to Set Up and Run: Setting up and running "The Bachelor" and "The Bachelorette" involves a comprehensive process. Contestants are selected through auditions and casting, and they participate in various dating activities and rose ceremonies. The shows also cover travel expenses for contestants on international dates and often feature engagement rings as part of the costs.

Legacy: "The Bachelor" and "The Bachelorette" have had a significant legacy in the dating reality show genre. They set the standard for dating competition shows and popularized the concept of rose ceremonies, where contestants receive roses to continue in the competition. The shows have been influential in shaping the format of dating shows on television.

Additionally, the franchise has spawned numerous spin-offs and specials, creating a Bachelor Nation community of fans. These spin-offs include "Bachelor in Paradise," where former contestants from "The Bachelor" and "The Bachelorette" meet in a tropical setting, and "Bachelor Pad," which features competitions and eliminations.

Detailed Description of the Shows: "The Bachelor" and "The Bachelorette" are dating competition reality TV shows that follow a similar format:

The Bachelor: In "The Bachelor," a single bachelor is introduced, and a group of eligible women competes for his affections. The bachelor goes on one-on-one dates and group dates with the contestants. At the end of each episode, he presents roses to the women he wishes to keep in the competition. The season concludes with a proposal or a commitment to a relationship.

The Bachelorette: "The Bachelorette" follows a similar format, but with a single bachelorette and a group of eligible men competing for her affections. The bachelorette goes on dates with the contestants and presents roses to those she wishes to keep.

Both shows include dramatic moments, emotional conversations, and interpersonal conflicts as contestants vie for the lead's attention and affection. The goal is to find love and a lasting relationship.

The shows are known for their dramatic rose ceremonies, where contestants who do not receive a rose are eliminated from the competition. "The Bachelor" and "The Bachelorette" also often feature international travel, extravagant dates, and heartfelt proposals.

Please note that "The Bachelor" and "The Bachelorette" may have continued to produce new seasons or spin-offs since my last research. For the most up-to-date information on these shows, you may refer to official sources or network websites where the shows are available.

The Amazing Race

Number of Episodes or Years of Production: "The Amazing Race" is a reality TV competition show that first premiered in 2001. It has had multiple seasons, with each season consisting of multiple episodes. The show's concept of teams racing around the world has been adapted in various countries, leading to a global franchise.

Costs of Production: The costs of production for "The Amazing Race" are significant due to the show's international scope. Expenses include travel costs for contestants and the production crew, filming permits and logistics in various countries, production crew salaries, challenges and tasks, and the grand prize awarded to the winning team.

Number of Viewers: "The Amazing Race" has consistently attracted a dedicated viewership over the years. The show's combination of adventure, travel, and teamwork appeals to a diverse audience. While viewership numbers can vary by season, it has maintained a loyal fan base.

Costs to Set Up and Run: Setting up and running "The Amazing Race" involves complex logistics. Contestants are selected through auditions, and the show covers their travel expenses to international destinations. Challenges and tasks are designed to test teams' physical and mental abilities, adding to the costs.

Legacy: "The Amazing Race" has had a significant legacy in the reality TV competition genre. It is known for showcasing global travel, adventure, and teamwork. The show's format of teams racing around the world has been emulated in various international versions, making it a successful global franchise.

Additionally, "The Amazing Race" has inspired viewers to explore different cultures and destinations, promoting the idea of adventure and exploration. It has also highlighted the importance of teamwork and communication in achieving common goals.

Detailed Description of the Show: "The Amazing Race" is a reality TV competition show that features teams of two racing around the world. The show typically follows a structured format:

Teams: Teams are composed of two individuals, often with pre-existing relationships (such as friends, family members, or couples).

Destinations: Teams travel to multiple international destinations, each with its own unique challenges and cultural experiences. The destinations can range from bustling cities to remote and challenging locations.

Challenges: At each destination, teams must complete various challenges and tasks that test their physical abilities, problem-solving skills, and teamwork. Challenges can include navigating unfamiliar environments, completing physical tasks, solving puzzles, and interacting with local residents.

Detours and Roadblocks: Teams often face choices in challenges, known as detours, where they must choose between two tasks with varying degrees of difficulty. Roadblocks are tasks that only one team member can perform.

Pit Stops: Teams race to reach designated pit stops at the end of each leg. The last team to arrive at the pit stop may face elimination.

Eliminations and Prizes: Teams are progressively eliminated as the race progresses. The final team to reach the finish line wins a grand prize, which can include a substantial cash reward.

"The Amazing Race" is known for its fast-paced and competitive nature, stunning travel destinations, and the personal stories and dynamics of the participating teams. It encourages viewers to dream of international travel and appreciate the beauty and diversity of the world.

Please note that "The Amazing Race" may have continued to produce new seasons or special editions since my last research. For the most up-to-date information on the show, you may refer to official sources or network websites where the show is available.

RuPaul's Drag Race

Number of Episodes or Years of Production: "RuPaul's Drag Race" is a reality TV competition show that first premiered in 2009. It has had multiple seasons, with each season consisting of multiple episodes. The show's format, which involves drag queens competing in various challenges, has gained popularity and led to international adaptations.

Costs of Production: The costs of production for "RuPaul's Drag Race" include the production crew salaries, the set design for the runway and challenges, costume and makeup expenses for contestants, guest judge appearances, and the prize awarded to the winning queen, which may include a cash prize and other opportunities.

Number of Viewers: "RuPaul's Drag Race" has garnered a dedicated and growing viewership over the years. The show has resonated with audiences interested in drag culture, LGBTQ+ representation, and the art of drag. Viewer numbers can vary by season, but it has maintained a strong fan base.

Costs to Set Up and Run: Setting up and running "RuPaul's Drag Race" involves a thorough casting process to select drag queens from diverse backgrounds and styles. Contestants compete in a variety of challenges, including fashion design, performance, and acting, which may require additional costume and prop expenses.

Legacy: "RuPaul's Drag Race" has had a profound legacy in elevating drag culture and championing LGBTQ+ visibility in mainstream media. The show has become a cultural phenomenon and has introduced drag queens to a global audience. Its impact extends beyond entertainment and has contributed to greater acceptance and understanding of drag as an art form.

Additionally, "RuPaul's Drag Race" has inspired a new generation of drag performers and artists. It has created a platform for drag queens to showcase their talent, creativity, and unique personas. The show has also fostered discussions on identity, self-expression, and the importance of authenticity.

Detailed Description of the Show: "RuPaul's Drag Race" is a reality TV competition show hosted by the iconic drag queen RuPaul. The show typically follows a structured format:

Contestants: Drag queens from diverse backgrounds and styles compete in the competition. Each queen adopts a persona and stage name for the duration of the show.

Challenges: Contestants compete in a series of challenges that test their skills in various aspects of drag, including fashion, makeup, performance, acting, and comedy. Challenges can range from creating runway looks to acting in scripted scenes.

Runway: One of the highlights of each episode is the runway, where contestants showcase their drag looks based on specific themes or categories. RuPaul and a panel of judges critique their performances.

Lip Sync for Your Life: At the end of each episode, contestants who perform the weakest in the challenge may have to "lip sync for their life" to a song. The winner stays in the competition, while the loser may be eliminated.

Guest Judges: Each episode features guest judges from the entertainment and fashion industries, adding to the variety of perspectives and critiques.

Prizes: The winner of "RuPaul's Drag Race" receives a grand prize that can include a cash prize, a supply of cosmetics, and other opportunities to further their drag career.

"RuPaul's Drag Race" is known for its celebration of self-expression, individuality, and the art of drag. It has introduced audiences to the diverse and vibrant world of drag culture, and it has become a platform for queens to gain recognition and pursue their careers.

For the most up-to-date information on the show, you may refer to official sources or network websites where the show is available.

40 ideas for new reality TV shows with names and descriptions:

"Eco Warriors Challenge"

Description: Contestants compete in eco-friendly challenges to promote sustainability and environmental awareness.

"Chef's Showdown"

Description: Amateur chefs face off in a culinary competition where they have to create gourmet dishes using limited ingredients.

"Home Makeover Extravaganza"

Description: Teams of designers and builders transform rundown homes into dream houses in record time.

"Escape Room Race"

Description: Contestants solve puzzles and riddles in various escape rooms, racing against the clock for cash prizes.

"Dance Off: Generation Clash"

Description: Dancers of different age groups compete in dance battles to prove that talent knows no age limit.

"Wilderness Survival Challenge"

Description: Individuals are dropped in remote wilderness locations and must survive with limited resources and skills.

"Adventure Couples"

Description: Couples embark on adrenaline-pumping adventures around the world, testing their bond and teamwork.

"Artistic Showdown"

Description: Artists of all mediums compete in creative challenges, from painting and sculpture to performance art.

"Tech Innovators"

Description: Tech-savvy contestants pitch and develop innovative tech solutions with mentorship from industry experts.

"Extreme Home Renovation"

Description: Teams take on extreme home renovations, from treehouse transformations to underwater dwellings.

"Reality Detective"

Description: Contestants solve real-life mysteries and crimes in a thrilling competition.

"Gardening Showdown"

Description: Green thumbs compete in gardening challenges to create stunning landscapes and gardens.

"Paranormal Investigators"

Description: Teams of paranormal enthusiasts investigate haunted locations to uncover supernatural mysteries.

"World's Toughest Jobs"

Description: Contestants take on grueling and dangerous jobs from around the world to win cash prizes.

"Epic Road Trip Challenge"

Description: Teams embark on cross-country road trips with a limited budget and a series of challenges along the way.

"Inventor's Showdown"

Description: Inventors pitch their groundbreaking inventions to a panel of judges in hopes of securing funding.

"Adrenaline Junkies"

Description: Thrill-seekers tackle extreme sports and stunts in a quest for the title of ultimate adrenaline junkie.

"Time Travel Experiment"

Description: Contestants are transported to different historical eras and must adapt to survive in the past.

"Artisan Craftsmen"

Description: Skilled artisans showcase their craftsmanship in challenges that range from blacksmithing to glassblowing.

"Ultimate Food Truck Challenge"

Description: Food truck owners compete in cooking challenges and entrepreneurial tasks to expand their businesses.

"Museum Heist"

Description: Teams plan and execute elaborate heists to retrieve valuable artifacts from fictional museums.

"Ghost Town Revival"

Description: Contestants restore and revitalize abandoned ghost towns, turning them into thriving communities.

"Disaster Survival"

Description: Participants experience simulated natural disasters and must use their survival skills to escape.

"Undercover Boss: Celebrity Edition"

Description: Celebrities go undercover in their own industries to experience the challenges faced by their employees.

"High-Stakes Poker Tournament"

Description: Poker enthusiasts compete in high-stakes tournaments for a chance to win big.

"Escape to the Wilderness"

Description: Urbanites leave behind their city lives to survive in the wilderness with basic supplies.

"Ghost Hunting Challenge"

Description: Contestants hunt for paranormal activity in haunted locations, facing their fears to win prizes.

"Extreme Weather Chasers"

Description: Teams chase extreme weather phenomena, providing valuable data and thrilling experiences.

"Fashion Design Showdown"

Description: Aspiring fashion designers create runway-worthy looks under tight deadlines and budget constraints.

"Culinary Around the World"

Description: Chefs from different cultures compete to showcase their cuisines in a culinary world tour.

"Virtual Reality Challenge"

Description: Contestants enter virtual reality worlds and complete challenges in immersive gaming environments.

"Crypto Treasure Hunt"

Description: Contestants solve crypto puzzles and riddles to find hidden cryptocurrency prizes.

"Ocean Exploration"

Description: Teams explore the depths of the ocean, uncovering underwater mysteries and marine life.

"Jungle Survival School"

Description: Novices learn survival skills from experts in the challenging environments of jungles and rainforests.

"Historical Re-enactment Show"

Description: Contestants immerse themselves in historical eras, living and competing as if they were in the past.

"Build Your Dream Home"

Description: Aspiring homeowners compete to design and build their dream homes with limited budgets.

"Epic Photography Challenge"

Description: Photographers capture stunning images in challenging locations and scenarios.

"Crypto Trading Showdown"

Description: Crypto traders compete in a trading competition with real investments and market challenges.

"Urban Exploration Race"

Description: Teams race through urban environments, solving puzzles and completing challenges in hidden locations.

"Space Pioneers"

Description: Contestants undergo astronaut training and compete for a chance to experience space travel.

These ideas cover a wide range of themes and concepts, offering exciting and diverse possibilities for new reality TV shows.

Dear valued reader, your feedback is invaluable! After reading my book, please take a moment to leave a review. Your thoughts help me grow as an author. Thank you!

Made in the USA
Las Vegas, NV
11 December 2024

13825142R00031